North Dakota Department of Public Instruction

**The General School Laws of the State of North Dakota**

North Dakota Department of Public Instruction

**The General School Laws of the State of North Dakota**

ISBN/EAN: 9783744666886

Printed in Europe, USA, Canada, Australia, Japan

Cover: Foto ©Suzi / pixelio.de

More available books at **www.hansebooks.com**

# THE GENERAL SCHOOL LAWS

OF THE

# STATE OF NORTH DAKOTA

COMPRISING ALL THE LAWS IN FORCE

PERTAINING TO PUBLIC SCHOOLS, STATE EDUCATIONAL INSTITUTIONS,
SCHOOL LANDS AND PUBLIC LANDS APPROPRIATED TO
THE USE OF THE STATE EDUCATIONAL
INSTITUTIONS, WITH

## .....APPENDICES.....

COMPILED AT THE OFFICE OF THE

## SUPERINTENDENT OF PUBLIC INSTRUCTION

January 1, 1896.

## PUBLISHED BY AUTHORITY

GRAND FORKS, N. D.:
HERALD, STATE PRINTERS AND BINDERS
1896.

## THIS VOLUME IS STATE PROPERTY.

*And is for the use of the*............ ........ .............................*of*

...... . ..................... .... ..................... .. .....*School District*.. ..................................................,

*County of*......... ... ............. ... .......................... , *State of North Dakota.*

---

School officers on retiring from office, are required by law to deliver this volume, with all other books and documents of an official character, to their successors in office.

# CONTENTS.

## PROVISIONS OF THE ENABLING ACT.

Public Schools_____ 9
School Lands_____ 9, 10
Lands for Public Institutions_____10, 11

## CONSTITUTIONAL PROVISIONS.

Article  2  The Legislative Department_____ 13
Article  3  Executive Department_____ 13
Article  5  Elective Franchise_____ 14
Article  8  Education _____ 14
Article  9  School and Public Lands_____ 15
Article 12  Public Debt and Public Works_____ 18
Article 19  Public Institutions_____ 19

## STATUTORY PROVISIONS.

### PART I.—PUBLIC SCHOOLS.
#### (Chapter 9, Political Code.)

Article  1  Superintendent of Public Instruction_____ 23
Article  2  County Superintendent of Schools_____ 26
Article  3  School Districts_____ 30
Article  4  Election of School Officers_____ 34
Article  5  Organization, Meetings and Duties of District Officers_____ 37
Article  6  Powers and Duties of District School Boards_____ 40
Article  7  School Funds_____ 46
Article  8  Taxes_____ 50
Article  9  Vacancies _____ 53
Article 10  Equalization of Indebtedness_____ 54
Article 11  Examinations and Certificates_____ 55
Article 12  Duties of Teachers_____ 59
Article 13  Institutes, Associations and Reading Circle_____ 61
Article 14  Compulsory Attendance_____ 63
Article 15  Fines, Forfeitures and Penalties_____ 65
Article 16  Bonds _____ 66
Article 17  Special Districts_____ 70
Article 18  Independent School Districts_____ 81
Article 19  Boards of Education in Certain Cities_____ 88
Article 20  Free Text Books_____ 90
Article 21  Purchase of Flags for School Districts_____ 91
Article 22  State Educational Library_____ 91
Article 23  High School Board_____ 91
Article 24  Health and Decency in Public Schools_____ 93

## PART II.—EDUCATIONAL INSTITUTIONS.
### (Chapter 10, Political Code.)

Article 25  University of North Dakota............................... 94
Article 26  Normal Schools..................................... 101
Article 27  North Dakota Academy of Science................... 105
Article 28  Agricultural College.............................. 107
Article 29  Deaf and Dumb Asylum.............................. 111
Article 30  Blind Asylum...................................... 114
Article 31  Industrial School................................. 116
Article 32  Lignite Coal to be Used........................... 118

## PART III.—SCHOOL AND PUBLIC LANDS.
### (Chapter 4, Political Code.)

Article 33  Board of University and School Lands.............. 119

## APPENDICES.

Appendix A—Special Laws.................................... 139
Appendix B—Laws Pertaining to Speculation in Office and Penalty for Failure
    to Make Reports, Blanks to be Furnished.............. 140
Appendix C—Filing Bond of Treasurer....................... 141
Appendix D—Bonds for Labor and Material for Public Buildings.............. 141
Appendix E—Digest of Decisions of Supreme Court........... 142
Appendix F—School Calendar................................ 148

# INTRODUCTORY.

This compilation of the General School Laws is authorized by the provisions of section 631 of the Political Code, 1895, (§ 10, Ch. 62, 1890,) and is designed to include all the congressional, constitutional and statutory provisions relating to education at present in force which, taken together, make the laws governing the complete school system of the State. It embraces the laws pertaining to the public schools, the State educational institutions, and the lands appropriated to the use of the public schools and the State educational institutions.

The compilation contains all general laws in full as revised in the code. Special acts are referred to by title only.

All laws herein contained are in full force and effect from and after January 1, 1896.

Special laws, designated by title only, laws pertaining to speculation in office and to penalty for failure to make reports, the filing of bond of school district treasurer, bonds for labor and' material for public buildings and the decisions of the Supreme Court of the Territory of Dakota and of the State of North Dakota pertaining to school matters are to be found in the appendices.

A calendar will also be found in the appendices which may be of assistance to school officers in the timely discharge of their duties.

EMMA F. BATES,
*Superintendent of Public Instruction.*

Department of Public Instruction, State of North Dakota,
Bismarck, January 1st, 1896.

# STATE OF NORTH DAKOTA.

—

## PROVISIONS OF THE ENABLING ACT.

—. —— -

§ 4. * * * And said (constitutional) conventions shall provide by ordinances irrevocable without the consent of the United States and the people of said states: * * *

Fourth. That provisions shall be made for the establishment and maintenance of systems of public schools, which shall be open to all children from said states, and free from sectarian control.

§ 10. That upon the admission of each of said states into the Union, sections numbered 16 and 36 in every township of said proposed states, and where such sections or any parts thereof have been sold or otherwise disposed of by or under the authority of any act of Congress, other lands equivalent thereto, in legal sub-divisions of not less than one-quarter section, and as contiguous as may be to the section in lieu of which the same is taken, are hereby granted to said states for the support of common schools, such indemnity lands to be selected within said states in such manner as the legislature may provide, with the approval of the Secretary of the Interior; *Provided*, That the sixteenth and thirty-sixth sections embraced in permanent reservations for national purposes shall not, at any time, be subject to the grants nor to the indemnity provisions of this act, nor shall any lands embraced in Indian, military or other reservations of any character, be sub-ject to the grants or to the indemnity provisions of this act until the reservation shall have been extinguished and such lands be restored to, and become a part of the public domain.

§ 11. That all lands herein granted for educational purposes shall be disposed of only at public sale, and at a price not less than ten (10) dollars per acre, the proceeds to constitute a per-manent school fund, the interest of which only shall be expended in the support of said schools. But said lands may, under such regulation as the Legislature shall prescribe, be leased for periods of not more than five years, in quantities not exceeding one section to any one person or company; and such lands shall not be subject to pre-emption, homestead entry, or any other entry under the land laws of the United States, whether surveyed or unsurveyed, but shall be reserved for school purposes only.

§ 13. That 5 per centum of the proceeds of the sales of public lands lying within said states which shall be sold by the United States subsequent to the admission of said states into the Union, after deducting all the expenses incident to the same, shall be paid to the said states, to be used as a permanent fund, the interest of which only shall be expended for the support of common schools within said states, respectively.

§ 14. That the lands granted to the Territories of Dakota and Montana by the act of February 18, 1881, entitled "An Act to Grant Lands to Dakota, Montana, Arizona, Idaho and Wyoming for University Purposes," are hereby vested in the States of South Dakota, North Dakota and Montana, respectively, if such states are admitted into the Union as provided in this act, to the extent of the full quantity of seventy-two sections to each of said states, and any portion of said lands that may not have been selected by either of said Territories of Dakota or Montana may be selected by the respective states aforesaid; but said act of February 18, 1881, shall be so amended as to provide that none of said lands shall be sold for less than ten (10) dollars per acre, and the proceeds shall constitute a permanent fund to be safely invested and held by said states severally, and the income thereof to be used exclusively for university purposes.   *   *   * None of the lands granted in this section shall be sold for less than ten (10) dollars per acre; but said lands may be leased in the same manner as provided in Section 11 of this act. The schools, colleges and universities provided for in this act shall forever remain under the exclusive control of said states, respectively, and no part of the proceeds arising from the sale or disposal of any lands herein granted for educational purposes shall be used for the support of any sectarian or denominational school, college or university.

§ 16. That 90,000 acres of land to be selected and located as provided in Section 10 of this act, are hereby granted to each of said states except to the State of South Dakota, to which 120,000 acres are granted, for the use and support of agricultural colleges in said states, as provided in the acts of Congress making donations of lands for such purposes.

§ 17. That in lieu of the grant of land for purposes of internal improvement made to new states by the eighth section of the act of September 4, 1841, which act is hereby repealed as to the states provided for by this act, and in lieu of any claim or demand by the said states, or either of them, under the act of September 28,

1850, and Section 2479 of the Revised Statutes, making a grant of swamp and overflowed lands to certain states, which grant it is hereby declared is not extended to the states provided for in this act, and in lieu of any grant of saline lands to said states, the following grants of land are hereby made, to-wit:

To the State of South Dakota: For the School of Mines, 40,000 acres; for the Reform School, 40,000 acres; for the Deaf and Dumb Asylum, 40,000 acres; for the Agricultural College, 40,000 acres; for the University, 40,000 acres; for the State Normal Schools, 80,000 acres; for public buildings at the capital of said State, 50,000 acres, and for such other educational and charitable purposes as the Legislature of said State may determine, 170,000 acres, in all, 500,000 acres.

To the State of North Dakota a like quantity of land as is in this section granted to the State of South Dakota, and to be for like purposes, and in like proportion as far as practicable.   *   *   *   That the states provided for in this act shall not be entitled to any further or other grants of land for any purpose than as expressly provided for in this act.   The lands granted by this section shall be held, appropriated and disposed of exclusively for the purposes herein mentioned, in such manner as the Legislatures of the respective states may severally provide.

§ 18.   That all mineral lands shall be exempted from the grants of this act.   But if sections 16 and 36, or any subdivision or portion of any smallest subdivision thereof in any township shall be found by the Department of the Interior to be mineral lands, said states are hereby authorized and empowered to select, in legal subdivisions, an equal quantity of other unappropriated lands in said states, in lieu thereof, for the use and the benefit of the common schools of said states.

§ 19.   That all lands granted in quantity or as indemnity by this act shall be selected, under the direction of the Secretary of the Interior, from the surveyed, unreserved and unappropriated public lands of the United States within the limits of the respective states entitled thereto.   And there shall be deducted from the number of acres of land donated by this act for specific objects to said states the number of acres in each heretofore donated by Congress to said territories for similar objects.

# CONSTITUTIONAL PROVISIONS.

(Adopted October 1, 1889.)

## PREAMBLE.

We, the people of North Dakota, grateful to Almighty God for the blessings of civil and religious liberty, do ordain and establish this Constitution.

## ARTICLE II.

### THE LEGISLATIVE DEPARTMENT.

§ 69. The Legislative Assembly shall not pass local or special laws in any of the following enumerated cases, that is to say:
\*         \*         \*         \*         \*         \*

12. Providing for the management of common schools.

## ARTICLE III.

### EXECUTIVE DEPARTMENT.

§ 82. There shall be chosen by the qualified electors of the State at the time and places of choosing members of the Legislative Assembly a   \*   \*   \*   Superintendent of Public Instruction,   \*   \*   \*   who shall have attained the age of twenty-five years, shall be a citizen of the United States, and shall have the qualifications of State electors. They shall severally hold their offices at the seat of government for the term of two years and until their successors are elected and duly qualified.
\*         \*         \*         \*         \*         \*         \*

§ 83. The powers and duties of the   \*   \*   Superintendent of Public Instruction,   \*   \*   shall be as prescribed by law.

§ 84. Until otherwise provided by law, the   \*   \*   \* Superintendent of Public Instruction   \*   \*   shall each receive an annual salary of $2,000;   \*   \*   but the salaries of any of the said officers shall not be increased or diminished during the period for which they shall have been elected, and all fees and profits arising from any of the said offices shall be covered into the State Treasury.

## ARTICLE V.

### ELECTIVE FRANCHISE.

§ 121. Every male person of the age of twenty-one years or upwards belonging to either of the following classes, who shall have resided in the State one year, in the county six months and in the precinct ninety days next preceding any election, shall be deemed a qualified elector at such election.

*First*—Citizens of the United States.

*Second*—Persons of foreign birth who shall have declared their intention to become citizens one year and not more than six years prior to such election, conformably to the naturalization laws of the United States.

*Third*—Civilized persons of Indian descent who shall have severed their tribal relation two years next preceding such election.

§ 123. Electors shall in all cases except treason, felony, breach of the peace or illegal voting, be privileged from arrest on the days of election during their attendance at, going to and returning from such election, and no elector shall be obliged to perform military duty on the day of election except in time of war or public danger.

§ 125. No elector shall be deemed to have lost his residence in this State by reason of his absence on business of the United States or of this State, or in the military or naval service of the United States.

§ 126. No soldier, seaman or marine in the army or navy of the United States shall be deemed a resident of this State in consequence of his being stationed therein.

§ 127. No person who is under guardianship, *non compos mentis* or insane, shall be qualified to vote at any election, nor shall any person convicted of treason or felony, unless restored to civil rights.

§ 128. Any woman having qualifications enumerated in Section 121 of this article as to age, residence and citizenship, and including those now qualified by the laws of the Territory, may vote for all school officers, and upon all questions pertaining solely to school matters, and be eligible to any school office.

§ 129. All elections by the people shall be by secret ballot subject to such regulations as shall be provided by law.

## ARTICLE VIII.

### EDUCATION.

§ 147. A high degree of intelligence, patriotism, integrity and morality on the part of every voter in a government by the people being necessary in order to insure the continuance of that government and the prosperity and happiness of the people, the

Legislative Assembly shall make provision for the establishment and maintenance of a system of public schools which shall be open to all children of the State of North Dakota, and free from sectarian control. The legislative requirement shall be irrevocable without the consent of the United States and the people of North Dakota.

§ 148. The Legislative Assembly shall provide at its first session after the adoption of this Constitution for a uniform system of free public schools throughout the State; beginning with the primary and extending through all grades up to and including the normal and collegiate course.

§ 149. In all schools instruction shall be given as far as practicable in those branches of knowledge that tend to impress upon the mind the vital importance of truthfulness, temperance, purity, public spirit, and respect for honest labor of every kind.

§ 150. A superintendent of schools for each county shall be elected every two years, whose qualifications, duties, powers and compensation shall be fixed by law.

§ 151. The Legislative Assembly shall take such other steps as may be necessary to prevent illiteracy, secure a reasonable degree of uniformity in course of study and to promote industrial, scientific and agricultural improvement.

§ 152. All colleges, universities and other educational institutions, for the support of which lands have been granted to this State, or which are supported by a public tax, shall remain under the absolute and exclusive control of the State. No money raised for the support of the public schools of the State shall be appropriated to or used for the support of any sectarian school.

## ARTICLE IX.

### SCHOOL AND PUBLIC LANDS.

§ 153. All proceeds of the public lands that have heretofore been or may hereafter be granted by the United States for the support of the common schools in this State; all such per centum as may be granted by the United States on the sale of public lands; the proceeds of property that shall fall to the State by escheat; the proceeds of all gifts and donations to the State for common schools, or not otherwise appropriated by the terms of the gift, and all other property otherwise acquired for common schools, shall be and remain a perpetual fund for the maintenance of the common schools of the State. It shall be deemed a trust fund, the principal of which shall forever remain inviolate, and may be increased but never diminished. The State shall make good all losses thereof.

§ 154. The interest and income of this fund, together with the net proceeds of all fines for violation of State laws, and all other sums which may be added thereto by law, shall be faithfully used and applied each year for the benefit of the common schools of the State, and shall be for this purpose apportioned among and between all the several common school corporations of the State in proportion to the number of children in each of school age, as may be fixed by law, and no part of the fund shall ever be diverted even temporarily from this purpose; or used for any other purpose whatever than the maintenance of common schools for the equal benefit of all the people of the State; *Provided, however,* That if any portion of the interest or income aforesaid be not expended during any year, said portion shall be added to and become a part of the school fund.

§ 155. After one year from the assembling of the First Legislative Assembly, the lands granted to the State from the United States for the support of the common schools, may be sold upon the following conditions, and no other: No more than one-fourth of all such lands shall be sold within the first five years after the same become saleable by virtue of this section. No more than one-half of the remainder within ten years after the same become saleable as aforesaid. The residue may be sold at any time after the expiration of said ten years. The Legislative Assembly shall provide for the sale of all school lands subject to the provisions of this article. The coal lands of the State shall never be sold, but the Legislative Assembly may by general laws provide for leasing of the same; the words "coal lands" shall include lands bearing lignite coal.

§ 156. The Superintendent of Public Instruction, Governor, Attorney General, Secretary of State and State Auditor shall constitute a board of commissioners, which shall be denominated the "Board of University and School Lands," and subject to the provisions of this article and any law that may be passed by the Legislative Assembly, said board shall have control of the appraisement, sale, rental and disposal of all school and university lands, and shall direct the investment of the funds arising therefrom in the hands of the State Treasurer, under the limitations of Section 160 of this article.

§ 157. The county superintendent of common schools, the chairman of the county board and the county auditor shall constitute boards of appraisal, and under the authority of the State Board of University and School Lands shall appraise all school lands within their respective counties, which they may from time to time recommend for sale at their actual value, under the prescribed terms, and shall first select and designate for sale the most valuable lands.

§ 158. No land shall be sold for less than the appraised value, and in no case for less than ten (10) dollars per acre. The purchaser shall pay one-fifth of the price in cash, and the remaining four-fifths as follows: One-fifth in five years, one-fifth in ten years, one-fifth in fifteen years and one-fifth in twenty years, with interest at the rate of not less than 6 per centum, payable annually in advance. All sales shall be held at the county seat of the county in which the land to be sold is situate, and shall be at public auction, and to the highest bidder, after sixty days' advertisement of the same in a newspaper of general circulation in the vicinity of the lands to be sold, and one at the seat of government. Such lands as shall not have been specially subdivided shall be offered in tracts of one-quarter section, and those so subdivided in the smallest subdivisions. All lands designated for sale and not sold within two years after appraisal shall be reappraised before they are sold. No grant or patent for any such lands shall issue until payment is made for the same; *Provided,* That the lands contracted to be sold by the State shall be subject to taxation from the date of such contract. In case the taxes assessed against any of said lands for any year remain unpaid until the the first Monday in October of the following year, then and thereupon the contract of sale for such lands shall become null and void.

§ 159. All lands, money or other property, donated, granted or received from the United States or any other source for a university, school of mines, reform school, agricultural college, deaf and dumb asylum, normal school, or other educational or charitable institution or purpose, and the proceeds of all such lands and other property so received from any source, shall be and remain perpetual funds, the interest and income of which together with the rents of all such lands as may remain unsold, shall be inviolably appropriated and applied to the specific objects of the original grants or gifts. The principal of every such fund may be increased but shall never be diminished, and the interest and income only shall be used. Every such fund shall be deemed a trust fund held by the State, and the State shall make good all losses thereof.

§ 160. All lands mentioned in the preceding section shall be appraised and sold in the same manner and under the same limitations and subject to all the conditions as to price and sale as provided above for the appraisal and sale of lands for the benefit of common schools; but a distinct and separate account shall be kept by the proper officers of each of said funds; *Provided,* That the limitations as to the time in which school land may be sold shall apply only to lands granted for the support of common schools.

§ 161. The Legislative Assembly shall have authority to provide by law for the leasing of lands granted to the State for educational and charitable purposes; but no such law shall authorize the leasing of said lands for a longer period than five years. Said land shall only be leased for pasturage and meadow purposes, and at a public auction after notice as heretofore provided in case of sale; *Provided,* That all of said school lands now under cultivation may be leased at the discretion and under the control of the Board of University and School Lands, for other than pasturage and meadow purposes until sold.    All rents shall be paid in advance.

§ 162.  The moneys of the permanent school fund and other educational funds shall be invested only in bonds of school corporations within the State, bonds of the United States, bonds of the State of North Dakota, or in first mortgages on farm lands in the State not exceeding in amount one-third of the actual value of any subdivision on which the same may be loaned, such value to be determined by the board of appraisers of school lands.

§ 163.  No law shall ever be passed by the Legislative Assembly granting to any person, corporation or association any privileges by reason of the occupation, cultivation or improvement of any public land by said person, corporation or association subsequent to the survey thereof by the general government. No claim for the occupation, cultivation or improvement of any public lands shall ever be recognized, nor shall such occupation, cultivation or improvement of any public lands ever be used to diminish, either directly or indirectly, the purchase price of said lands.

§ 165.  The Legislative Assembly shall pass suitable laws for the safe-keeping, transfer and disbursement of the school funds; and shall require all officers charged with the same or the safe keeping thereof to give ample bonds for all moneys and funds received by them, and if any of said officers shall convert to his own use in any manner or form, or shall loan with or without interest or shall deposit in his own name, or otherwise than in the name of the State of North Dakota, or shall deposit in any banks or with any person or persons, or exchange for other funds or property any portion of the school funds aforesaid, or purposely allow any portion of the same to remain in his own hands uninvested except in the manner prescribed by law, every such act shall constitute an embezzlement of so much of the aforesaid school funds as shall be thus taken or loaned, or deposited, or exchanged, or withheld, and shall be a felony; and any failure to pay over, produce or account for the State school funds or any part of the same intrusted to any such officer, as by law required and demanded, shall be held and be taken to be *prima facie* evidence of such embezzlement.

## ARTICLE XII.

### PUBLIC DEBT AND PUBLIC WORKS.

§ 183.  The debt of any county, township, town, school district, or any other political subdivision, shall never exceed five (5) per centum upon the assessed value of the taxable property therein. *    *    *    In estimating the indebtedness which a city, county, township, school district or any other political subdivision may incur, the entire amount of existing indebtedness, whether

contracted prior or subsequent to the adoption of this Constitution, shall be included; * * * All bonds or obligations in excess of the amount of indebtedness permitted by this
constitution, given by any city, county, township, town, school
district, or any other political subdivision, shall be void.

§ 184. Any city, county, township, town, school district, or
any other political subdivision incurring indebtedness shall, at or
before the time of so doing, provide for the collection of an
annual tax sufficient to pay the interest and also the principal
thereof when due, and all laws or ordinances providing for the
payment of the interest or principal of any debt shall be irre-
pealable until such debt is paid.

§ 185. Neither the State nor any county, city, township, town
school district or any other political subdivision shall loan or
give its credit or make donations to or in aid of any individual,
association or corporation, except for necessary support of the
poor, nor subscribe to or become the owner of the capital stock
of any association or corporation, * * * * * *

§ 186. * * * No bills, claims, accounts or
demands against the State, or any county or other political subdivision, shall be audited, allowed or paid until a full itemized
statement in writing shall be filed with the officer or officers
whose duty it may be to audit the same.

§ 187. * * * * No bond or evidence of debt
of any county, or bond of any township or other political subdivision, shall be valid unless the same have indorsed thereon
a certificate signed by the county auditor, or other officer authorized by law to sign such certificate, stating that said bond, or
evidence of debt, is issued pursuant to law and is within the debt
limit.

## ARTICLE XIX.

### PUBLIC INSTITUTIONS.

§ 215. The following public institutions of the State are permanently located at the places hereinafter named, each to have
the lands specifically granted to it by the United States in the act
of Congress approved February 22, 1889, to be disposed of and
used in such manner as the Legislative Assembly may prescribe,
subject to the limitations provided in the article on school and
public lands contained in this Constitution: * * * *

*Second*--The State University and the School of Mines at the
city of Grand Forks, in the county of Grand Forks.

*Third*—The Agricultural College at the city of Fargo, in the
county of Cass.

*Fourth*—A State Normal School at the city of Valley City, in
the county of Barnes; and the Legislative Assembly in apportioning the grant of 80,000 acres of land for Normal Schools made in

the act of Congress referred to, shall grant to the said Normal School at Valley City aforementioned 50,000 acres, and said lands are hereby appropriated to said institution for that purpose.

*Fifth*—The Deaf and Dumb Asylum at the city ot Devils Lake in the county of Ramsey.

\*     \*     \*     \*     \*     \*     \*

*Seventh*—A State Normal School at the city of Mayville in the county of Traill; and the Legislative Assembly in apportioning the grant of land made by Congress in the act aforesaid for State Normal schools, shall assign 30,000 acres to the institution hereby located at Mayville, and said lands are hereby appropriated for said purpose.     \*     \*     \*     \*     \*     \*     \*

§ 216. The following named public institutions are hereby permanently located as hereinafter provided, each to have so much of the remaining grant of 170,000 acres of land made by the United States for "other educational and charitable institutions," as is allotted by law, viz.:

*Second*—A Blind Asylum, or such other institution as the Legislative Assembly may determine, at such place in the county of Pembina as the qualified electors of said county may determine at an election to be held as prescribed by the Legislative Assembly, with a grant of 30,000 acres.

*Third*—An Industrial School and School for Manual Training, or such other educational or charitable institution as the Legislative Assembly may provide, at the town of Ellendale, in the county of Dickey, with a grant of 40,000 acres.

*Fourth*—A School of Forestry, or such other institution as the Legislative Assembly may determine, at such place in one of the counties of McHenry, Ward, Bottineau, or Rolette as the electors of said counties may determine by an election for that purpose, to be held as provided by the Legislative Assembly.

*Fifth*—A Scientific School, or such other educational or charitable institution as the Legislative Assembly may prescribe, at the city of Wahpeton, county of Richland, with a grant of 40,000 acres; *Provided*, That no other institution of a character similar to any one of those located by this article shall be established or maintained without a revision of this Constitution.

# STATUTORY PROVISIONS.

## PART I.—PUBLIC SCHOOLS.

Article                                                                    Section.
1.   Superintendent of Public Instruction _____  ___   1-16
2.   County Superintendent of Schools _____   17-36
3.   School Districts _____   37-48
4.   Election of School Officers _____   49-57
5.   Organization, Meetings and Duties of District Officers _____   58-69
6.   Powers and Duties of District School Boards _____ _____  _____   70-88
7.   School Funds _____   89-99
8.   Taxes _____ _____  100-104
9.   Vacancies _____  105-109
10.  Equalization of Indebtedness _____ _____  110-114
11.  Examinations and Certificates _____  115-124
12.  Duties of Teachers _____  125-133
13.  Institutes, Associations and Reading Circle _____  134-137
14.  Compulsory Attendance _____  138-143
15.  Fines, Forfeitures and Penalties _____  144-153
16.  Bonds _____  154-163
17.  Special Districts _____  ..  ___164-206
18.  Independent School Districts _____  207-234
19.  Boards of Education in Certain Cities _____  235-241
20.  Free Text Books _____  242-243
21.  Purchase of Flags for School Districts _____   244
22.  State Educational Library _____   245
23.  High School Board _____  246-252
24.  Health and Decency in Public Schools _____   253

## PART II.—EDUCATIONAL INSTITUTIONS.

25.  University of North Dakota _____  254-283
26.  Normal Schools _____  284-301
27.  North Dakota Academy of Science _____  302-312
28.  Agricultural College _____  313-329
29.  Deaf and Dumb Asylum _____  330-345
30.  Blind Asylum ____ _____  346-352
31.  Industrial School _____  353-362
32.  Lignite Coal to be Used _____   363

## PART III—SCHOOL AND PUBLIC LANDS.

33.  Board of University and School Lands _____  364-430

# PART I.--PUBLIC SCHOOLS.

## ARTICLE I.

### SUPERINTENDENT OF PUBLIC INSTRUCTION.

Section.
1. Qualifications of—Term of Office.
2. To Preserve Miscellaneous Documents.
3. Supervision of Schools.
4. Prepare and Furnish School Supplies.
5. Examinations and Teachers' Certificates.
6. Prescribe Course of Study.
7. Rules for Teachers' Institutes.
8. Advise County Superintendents.

Section.
9. Record of Official Acts.
10. School Laws to be Printed.
11. Conference with County Superintendents.
12. Seal.
13. To Assist at Teachers' Institutes.
14. Biennial Report, What to Contain.
15. Reports to be Printed.
16. Salary, Traveling Expenses.

(Figures in paranthesis refer to section numbers in the Revised Codes.)

§ 1. (622.) QUALIFICATIONS OF. TERM OF OFFICE.] There shall be elected by the qualified electors of the state at the time of choosing members of the Legislative Assembly a Superintendent of Public Instruction, who shall have attained the age of twenty-five years, and who shall have the qualifications of an elector for that office and the holder of a State certificate of the highest grade, issued in some state, or a graduate of some reputable university, college or normal school. He shall hold his office at the seat of government for the term of two years commencing on the first Monday in January following his election and until his successor is elected and qualified.

§ 2. (623.) TO PRESERVE MISCELLANEOUS DOCUMENTS.] He shall preserve in his office all books, maps, charts, works on education, school reports and school laws of other states, and cities, plans for school buildings and other articles of educational interest and value which may come into his possession as such officer, and at the expiration of his term he shall deliver them together with the reports, statements, records and archives of his office to his successor.

§ 3. (624.) SUPERVISION OF SCHOOLS.] He shall have the general supervision of the public schools of the State and shall be ex-officio member of the Board of University and School Lands and of the Normal School Boards of the State.

§ 4. (625.) PREPARE AND FURNISH SCHOOL SUPPLIES.] He shall prepare, cause to be printed and furnished to the proper officer or persons all school registers, reports, statements, notices and returns needed or required to be used in the schools or by the school officers in the State. He shall prepare and furnish the school officers, through the county superintendents, lists of publications approved by him as suitable for district libraries;

such lists shall also contain the lowest price at which each publication can be purchased, and such other information relative to the purchase of district libraries as he may deem requisite.

§ 5. (626.) EXAMINATIONS AND TEACHERS' CERTIFICATES.] He shall prepare or cause to be prepared all questions to be used in the examination of applicants for teachers' certificates, prescribe the rules and regulations for conducting such examinations and issue or revoke State certificates as provided in this chapter.

§ 6. (627.) PRESCRIBE COURSE OF STUDY.] He shall prepare and prescribe a course of study for all the public and normal schools of the State and the course of study, training and practice of the professional department of schools, designated and supported wholly or in part by the State.

§ 7. (628.) RULES FOR TEACHERS' INSTITUTES.] He shall prescribe rules and regulations for the holding of teachers' institutes, and after counseling and advising with county superintendents, shall appoint conductors therefor. He shall prescribe the course of instruction for teachers' institutes, and the course of reading for the teachers' reading circles within the State.

§ 8. (629.) ADVISE COUNTY SUPERINTENDENTS.] He shall counsel with and advise county superintendents upon all matters involving the welfare of schools, and he shall, when requested, give them written answers to all questions concerning the school law. He shall decide all appeals from the decision of the county superintendents, and may for such decisions require affidavits, verified statements or sworn testimony as to the facts in issue. He shall prescribe and cause to be enforced rules of practice and regulations pertaining to the hearing and determination of appeals, and necessary for carrying into effect the school laws of the State.

§ 9. (630.) RECORD OF OFFICIAL ACTS.] He shall keep a complete record of all his official acts and shall file in his office all appeals and the papers pertaining thereto.

§ 10. (631.) SCHOOL LAWS TO BE PRINTED.] He shall at least once in two years cause to be printed the school laws of the State, with such notes and decisions thereon as may seem to him advisable, and shall furnish them as they are needed to the school officers in the State.

§ 11. (632.) CONFERENCE WITH COUNTY SUPERINTENDENTS.] He shall meet the county superintendents of each judicial district or of two or more districts combined at such time and place as he shall appoint, giving them due notice of such meeting. The objects of such meeting shall be to accumulate valuable facts relative to schools, to compare views, to discuss principles, to hear discussions and suggestions relative to the examinations and qualifications of teachers, methods of instruction, text books, institutes, visitation of schools and other matters relating to the public schools.

§ 12. (633.) SEAL.] He shall provide and keep a seal by which all his official acts may be authenticated.

§ 13. (634.) To ASSIST AT TEACHERS' INSTITUTES.] He shall when practicable, attend and assist at teachers' institutes and aid and encourage generally teachers in qualifying themselves for the successful discharge of their duties; he shall labor faithfully in all practicable ways for the welfare of the public schools of the State, and shall perform such other duties as shall be required of him by law.

§ 14. (635.) BIENNIAL REPORT, WHAT TO CONTAIN.] He shall, on or before the first day of November preceding the biennial session of the Legislative Assembly, make and transmit to the Governor a report, showing:

1. The number of school districts, schools, teachers employed and pupils taught therein and the attendance of pupils and studies pursued by them.

2. The financial condition of the schools, their receipts and expenditures, value of school houses and property, cost of tuition and wages of teachers

3. The condition, educational and financial, of the normal and higher institutions connected with the school system of the State and as far as it can be ascertained, of the private schools, academies and colleges in the State.

4. Such general matters, information and recommendations relating to the educational interests of the State as he may deem important.

§ 15. (636.) REPORTS TO BE PRINTED.] One thousand copies of the report of the Superintendent of Public Instruction shall be printed biennially in the month of December preceding the session of the Legislative Assembly. One copy shall be furnished to each of the members of the Legislative Assembly, one copy to each county superintendent of the State, one copy to the president of each school board, one copy to each State officer, one copy to each State and Territorial Superintendent and twenty copies shall be filed in the office of the Superintendent of Public Instruction and ten copies in the State library. The remaining copies shall be distributed among the various colleges, universities and other libraries of the United States.

§ 16. (637.) SALARY, TRAVELING EXPENSES.] He shall receive an annual salary of two thousand dollars and in addition thereto his actual and necessary traveling expenses incurred in the discharge of his official duties, not exceeding six hundred dollars in any one year, such expenses to be paid monthly on the warrant of the State Auditor upon his filing with such Auditor an itemized statement of such expenses properly verified.

## ARTICLE II.

### COUNTY SUPERINTENDENT OF SCHOOLS.

Section.
17. Election—Term of Office.
18. General Duties.
19. Visitation of Schools.
20. General Duties—Continued.
21. Record of Official Acts.
22. Meetings with School Officers.
23. To Decide Questions in Controversy.
24. Power to Administer Oaths.
25. Institute Fund, How Raised and Used.
26. Apportionment of State Tuition Fund.

Section.
27. Teacher's Certificate may be Revoked, when
28. Report to State Superintendent.
29. Appraisement of School Lands—Fees.
30. Office, Postage and Stationery.
31. Salary—Deputy—Traveling Expenses.
32. Qualifications of.
33. Shall not Engage in Teaching.
34. Shall not Absent Himself from County.
35. Subject to Removal.
36. Not Applicable in Every County.

§ 17. (638.) ELECTION. TERM OF OFFICE.] There shall be elected in each organized county at the same time other county officers are elected a county superintendent of schools, whose term of office shall be two years, commencing on the first Monday in January following his election and until his successor is elected and qualified.

§ 18. (639.) GENERAL DUTIES.] The county superintendent of schools shall have the general superintendence of the public schools in his county, except those in cities which are organized under special law and those in special or independent school districts.

§ 19. (640.) VISITATION OF SCHOOLS.] He shall visit each public school under his supervision. He shall at such visit carefully observe the condition of the school, the mental and moral instruction given, the methods of teaching employed by the teacher, the teacher's ability and the progress of the pupils. He shall advise and direct the teacher in regard to the instruction, classification, government and discipline of the school and the course of study. He shall keep a record of such visits and by memoranda indicate his judgment of the teacher's ability to teach and govern and the condition and progress of the school, which shall be open to inspection by any school director.

§ 20. (641.) GENERAL DUTIES CONTINUED.] He shall carry into effect all instructions of the Superintendent of Public Instruction given within his authority. He shall distribute to the proper officers and to teachers all blanks furnished him by such Superintendent, and needed by such officers and teachers. Acting under the instructions of the Superintendent of Public Instruction, he shall convene the teachers of his county at least one Saturday in each month during which the public schools are in progress, or if the distance is too great he may convene the teachers of two or more districts in each of the several portions of his county in county or district institutes, or teachers' circles for normal instruction and the study of methods of teaching, organizing, classifying and governing schools, and for such other instruction as may be set forth in the course of reading prescribed by the Superintendent of Public Instruction for the State

Teachers' Reading Circle. Each teacher shall attend the full session of such institute or circle and participate in the duties and exercises thereof or forfeit one day's wages for each day's absence therefrom, unless such absence is occasioned by sickness of the teacher or others to whom his attention is due; but when on account of distance or otherwise it would impose a hardship upon any teacher to attend, or would cause such teacher to neglect his school, the county superintendent may excuse such teacher from attendance.

§ 21. (642.) RECORD OF OFFICIAL ACTS.] He shall keep a record of all his official acts and shall preserve all books, maps, charts and apparatus sent him as a school officer, or belonging to his office. He shall file all reports and statements from teachers and school boards and shall turn them over to his successor in office.

§ 22. (643.) MEETINGS WITH SCHOOL OFFICERS.] He may arrange for meetings with school officers at designated times and places, due notice of which has been given, for the purpose of inspecting the district records and instructing in the manner of keeping the same and of preparing the reports of district officers. He shall visit the officers of the several school districts as often as may be necessary to secure the correct keeping of the records. He shall, on or before the first day of April in each year, prepare and furnish to the several assessors of the county a correct sectional map of their respective districts, showing the boundaries and names or numbers of all school districts therein.

§ 23. (644.) TO DECIDE QUESTIONS IN CONTROVERSY.] He shall decide all matters in controversy arising in his county in the administration of the school law or appealed to him from the decisions of school officers or boards. An appeal may be taken from his decision to the Superintendent of Public Instruction, in which case a full written statement of the facts, together with the testimony and his decision in the case shall be certified to the Superintendent of Public Instruction for his decision in the matter, which decision shall be final, subject to adjudication or the proper legal remedies in the courts.

§ 24. (645.) POWER TO ADMINISTER OATHS.] He shall have power to administer oaths of office to all subordinate school officers, and to witnesses and to examine them under oath in all controversies pending before him arising in the administration of the school laws; but he shall not receive pay for administering such oaths.

§ 25. (646.) INSTITUTE FUND, HOW RAISED AND USED.] All fees received by him for the examination of teachers shall be turned over to the county treasurer, who shall keep the same as a special fund to be known as the "institute fund" and which shall be used only for the expenses of holding county teachers' institutes, to be paid out upon proper warrants issued by the county auditor upon the sworn and itemized voucher of the county superintendent.

§ 26. (647.) APPORTIONMENT OF STATE TUITION FUND.] He shall make apportionment of the State tuition fund among the school corporations of the county, as provided in this chapter.

§ 27. (648.) TEACHER'S CERTIFICATE MAY BE REVOKED, WHEN.] He shall see that the pupils are instructed in the several branches of study required by law to be taught in the schools as far as they are qualified to pursue them. If any teacher neglects or refuses to give instruction as required by law in physiology and hygiene, and the nature and effect of alcoholic drinks, narcotics and stimulants, the county superintendent shall promptly revoke such teacher's certificate and cause him to be discharged. If the teacher, so neglecting or refusing to give instructions in such branches, holds a State certificate, the county superintendent shall immediately certify such refusal or neglect to the superintendent of public instruction.

§ 28. (649.) REPORT TO STATE SUPERINTENDENT.] He shall, on or before the fifteenth day of August in each year, make and transmit a report to the superintendent of public instruction, containing such statistics, items and statements relative to the schools of the county, as may be required by such superintendent. Such report shall be made upon and conform to the blanks furnished by the superintendent of public instruction for that purpose. He shall not be paid his salary for the last quarter of his official year, until he presents to the county commissioners, the receipt of the superintendent of public instruction for such annual report.

§ 29. (650.) APPRAISEMENT OF SCHOOL LANDS. FEES.] He shall perform such duties as appraiser of the school lands in his county, and also in the leasing and sale of such lands, as may be required of him by the Board of University and School Lands. He shall be paid for such services three dollars a day for the time actually employed therein and five cents a mile for the distance actually and necessarily traveled in the discharge of such duties, to be paid by the State Treasurer out of the funds appropriated for the current expenses of the Board of University and School Lands.

§ 30. (651.) OFFICE, POSTAGE AND STATIONERY.] He may provide for himself a suitable office for the transaction of official business when not provided therewith by the county commissioners, and such commissioners shall audit and pay his reasonable accounts for the use and furniture of such office. They shall also furnish him with all necessary books, stationery and postage; but not more than one hundred and twenty-five dollars a year shall be paid by any county for office rent, books, stationery, postage and furniture, and when an office room is furnished by the county he shall not be allowed to exceed fifty dollars a year for stationery and postage.

§ 31. (652.) SALARY. DEPUTY. TRAVELING EXPENSES.] The salary of the county superintendent of schools shall be as follows: In each county having one school and not over five, one hundred dollars; six schools and not over ten, two hundred dollars; eleven schools and not over fifteen, three hundred dollars; sixteen schools and not over twenty, four hundred dollars; twenty-one schools and not over twenty-five, five hundred dollars; twenty-six schools and not over thirty, six hundred dollars; thirty-one schools and not over thirty-five, seven hundred dollars; thirty six schools and not over forty, eight hundred dollars; forty-one schools and not over fifty, nine hundred dollars; and for each additional ten schools or major fraction thereof, one hundred dollars additional; *provided*, that in computing the salary of such superintendent no school shall be included unless the same shall have been taught at least three months during the preceding year; *provided, further*, that such salaries shall not exceed fifteen hundred dollars in any county. In addition thereto he shall receive seven cents a mile for the distance actually and necessarily traveled by him in the discharge of his duties. He shall at the end of every three months make and furnish to the county commissioners an itemized statement of the distance so traveled in the discharge of his duties, which shall be audited and ordered paid by the board of county commissioners. The amount of his salary shall be determined each year by the actual number of schools or separate departments in graded schools over which such superintendent had official supervision during the preceding year, and the same shall be paid out of the county general fund monthly upon the warrant of the county auditor. In each county which shall be organized for school purposes after the adoption of this code, the county superintendent shall be paid a salary at the rate of one hundred dollars a year until the first Monday in October next following his election, after which his salary shall be as provided for in this section. The county superintendent may appoint a deputy who shall perform the duties of the county superintendent during his absence from the county; but no additional salary shall be paid such deputy, except in counties having eighty or more schools, in which counties the board of county commissioners may appropriate not to exceed one hundred dollars each year for clerical assistance in the office. of the county superintendent, but such deputy shall be paid seven cents a mile for the distance actually and necessarily traveled by him, to be paid in the same manner the county superintendent is paid. The county superintendent shall be responsible for the official acts of such deputy.

§ 32. (653.) QUALIFICATIONS OF.] No person shall be deemed qualified for the office of county superintendent, unless he holds a certificate of the highest county grade or its equivalent.

§ 33. (654.) SHALL NOT ENGAGE IN TEACHING.] No county superintendent of schools, except as hereinafter provided, shall engage in teaching during the term for which he was elected, nor shall any person under contract to teach be qualified to hold the office of county superintendent of schools.

§ 34. (655.) SHALL NOT ABSENT HIMSELF FROM COUNTY.] No county superintendent of schools shall engage in any profession or occupation, nor shall he absent himself from the county or district for which he is elected to engage in any occupation, profession or pursuit during the term for which he is elected for such time and in such manner as to interfere with the proper discharge of his duties as county superintendent of schools.

§ 35. (656.) SUBJECT TO REMOVAL.] Any county superintendent of schools who neglects or violates any of the provisions of sections 654 and 655 shall be subject to removal from office.

§ 36. (657.) NOT APPLICABLE IN EVERY COUNTY.] None of the provisions of sections 654 and 655 shall be applicable to counties in which the salary of county superintendents of schools is less than twelve hundred dollars per annum.

## ARTICLE III.

### SCHOOL DISTRICTS.

Section.
37. What Constitutes a School Corporation.
38. School Township to Conform to Civil Township when Possible.
39. What Territory may be Organized into District School Corporations.
40. New School Districts, How Formed.
41. When School Corporations may be Divided and Attached to Other Districts.
42. Annexation of School Corporations.

Section.
43. When Civil Townships may Consolidate into School District.
44. School Districts, How Named.
45. When Boundaries to be Rearranged and Established and How.
46. Boundaries, How Changed in Future.
47. Rights and Powers of School Corporations.
48. Plats of School Districts to be Furnished by County Auditor.

§ 37. (658.) WHAT CONSTITUTES A SCHOOL CORPORATION.] Each civil township in the state, not organized for school purposes under the district system at the taking effect of this code, shall be and is hereby constituted a distinct school corporation, and whenever in any county a civil township shall hereafter be organized it shall from and after such organization be and constitute a distinct school corporation, except as otherwise specially provided in this chapter.

§ 38. (659.) SCHOOL TOWNSHIP TO CONFORM TO CIVIL TOWNSHIP WHEN POSSIBLE.] Each school township in every county in the state, which at the taking effect of this code consists of territory not organized into a civil township, shall be and remain a distinct school corporation; *provided*, that whenever such school township, or any part thereof, shall be organized into or annexed to a civil township, such civil township shall thenceforth constitute a distinct school corporation; but nothing in this section shall be construed to alter the boundary lines of any school township organized prior to the passage of this code, except upon petition as hereinafter provided.

§ 39. (660.) WHAT TERRITORY MAY BE ORGANIZED INTO DISTRICT SCHOOL CORPORATIONS.] The county commissioners of each county, not organized for school purposes under the district school system at the taking effect of this code, shall organize into a distinct school corporation any territory not, at the taking effect of this code, already organized into a civil township or a school township, upon being petitioned so to do by one-third of the residents of such territory, having the care and custody of any child of school age; *provided*, such territory shall consist of not less than one congressional township, having at least eight thousand dollars of taxable property and at least ten children of school age residing therein. The county commissioners of every such county, with the advice and consent of the county superintendent, may rearrange the boundaries in any school corporation whose territory is not included within a civil township, when petitioned so to do by a majority of the voters residing within such school corporation, whose boundaries will be effected thereby, subject to the same restrictions and conditions as to extent of territory, value of taxable property and number of resident children of school age as in the organization of a school corporation from territory not included in a civil township. In the formation of school corporations and the rearrangement of their boundaries as provided for in this section, the boundary lines of congressional townships shall be followed as far as possible as school corporation lines.

§ 40. (661.) NEW SCHOOL DISTRICTS, HOW FORMED.] In any county hereafter organized the county commissioners shall so divide the county or the parts thereof, which include every congressional township in such county which has residing therein not less than ten children of school age, into school corporations as will best promote the permanent interests of public schools in the county, upon the same petition and subject to the same condition and restrictions as are contained in section 660.

§ 41. (662.) WHEN SCHOOL CORPORATIONS MAY BE DIVIDED AND ATTACHED TO OTHER DISTRICTS.] If a portion of any such school corporation having not more than ten children of school age residing therein is separated from the other portion of such corporation by any natural obstacle which practically prevents such children from attending school in such other portion, the county commissioners of the county may annex such portion so separated to an adjoining school corporation, and the portion so annexed shall constitute a part of such adjacent corporation. If such adjacent corporation lies in another county, the county commissioners of the two counties may jointly make such annexation.

§ 42. (663.) ANNEXATION OF SCHOOL CORPORATIONS.] In any county not organized for school purposes under the district system at the taking effect of this code, if a town or village not organized into a special district is divided by a civil township line or if such town or village is divided by any county line, the county commissioners of such county, or the county commissioners of such adjacent counties acting in joint session, as the case may be, may when petitioned so to do by a majority of the voters of each part·of said town or village, annex one part of such town or village to the adjacent school corporation which includes the other part of such town or village and the part so annexed shall constitute a portion of such adjacent corporation.

§.43. (664.) WHEN CIVIL TOWNSHIPS MAY CONSOLIDATE INTO SCHOOL DISTRICT.] In any county not organized for school purposes under the district system at the taking effect of this code, if a civil township having less than fifteen persons of school age residing therein, by reason of the irregular course of natural boundary, contains less than twelve sections or square miles of territory, it shall constitute a portion of the adjacent school district with which it has the longest common boundary line.

§ 44. (665.) SCHOOL DISTRICTS, HOW NAMED.] Each school corporation constituted or formed under the provisions of this article, shall be designated a school district as distinguished from a civil township or congressional township and shall be named as follows:   Each school district which consists of a civil township shall be named "........school district of........county, State of North Dakota," with the name of the civil township which constitutes the districts inserted in the blank before the word "school" and the name of the county in which it is situated inserted before the word "county." Each school district which consists of territory not organized into a civil township but which has been named by a distinctive name shall have such distinctive name inserted in the blank before the word "school." Each school district consisting of territory not organized into a civil township which has no distinctive name shall be named "school district No....... of ........ county, State of North Dakota," with its proper number inserted in the blank after the word "number" and the proper name of the county inserted in the blank before the word "county;" *provided*, that in each county organized for school purposes under the district system at the taking effect of this code, the several school districts shall retain and be known by the number which they have respectively at the time of the taking effect of this code and any school district hereafter formed in any such county shall be known by the number next higher than that of the highest pre-existing numbered district.

§ 45. (666.) WHEN BOUNDARIES TO BE REARRANGED AND ESTABLISHED AND HOW.] The county commissioners and county superintendent of schools in each county, which at the taking effect of this code, is organized for school purposes under the district system, shall meet on the first Monday in May, A. D. 1896, at the place where the meetings of such commissioners are usually held and shall rearrange and establish the boundaries of the several school districts of the county unless the same has already been done, as follows:

1.  Each civil township in a county, no part of which is

included in a school district already organized, shall be formed into a single school district.

2. Each congressional township in the county, no part of which is included in a civil township nor in an organized school district, if it contains twelve or more persons of school age, shall be formed into a single school district.

3. All territory in a county situated in a civil township, part of which is organized into a school district or situated in a congressional township not included in a civil township, and a portion of which is organized into a school district shall be annexed to and form a part of the organized school district lying wholly or in part in such civil or congressional township.

4. Each school district now organized which has less than ten persons of school age residing therein shall be annexed to and form a part of such adjacent school district as shall be most convenient for such persons of school age, when in the judgment of such commissioners and superintendent such annexation can be made without detriment to the school or to the pupils residing in such district.

5. The boundary lines of each school district which lies partly within two or more civil townships shall be so changed that such school district shall lie wholly within one civil township, so far as in the judgment of such commissioners and superintendent such change can be made without detriment to the schools or to the pupils therein.

6. Such commissioners and superintendent shall make such changes generally in the boundary lines of the school districts of the county, not in their judgment detrimental to the interests of the schools of the county, as will reduce the number of school districts in the county, and form school districts not extending beyond the boundaries of the civil township.

§ 46. (667.) BOUNDARIES, HOW CHANGED IN FUTURE.] After the boundary lines of the several school districts in any of the counties are rearranged and established as provided for in the last section, or at any time thereafter, such boundary so established, or any boundary rearranged and established as aforesaid, may be changed by the county commissioners and superintendent of schools of such county at a regular meeting of the board, upon petition of three-fourths of the resident voters in and of the parts of districts to be included in any new districts, or of the parts of districts desiring such change; *provided*, that there are at least twelve children of school age within the boundaries proposed to be benefited by such change or creation of a new district, and it shall appear to the satisfaction of a majority of such board and to the county superintendent that such change will be beneficial to the schools and to the public; and *provided further*, that each congressional township not wholly or in part included in a civil township, and no portion of which is organized for school purposes, shall be formed into a school district as soon as it shall have residing therein twelve or more children of school age.

§ 47. (668.) RIGHTS AND POWERS OF SCHOOL CORPORATIONS.] Each school district constituted and formed as provided in this article shall be a distinct corporation, and under its proper name or number as such corporation, may sue and be sued, contract and be contracted with, and may acquire, purchase, hold and use personal or real property for school purposes or for the purposes mentioned in this chapter and sell and dispose of the same.

§ 48. (669.) PLATS OF SCHOOL DISTRICTS TO BE FURNISHED BY COUNTY AUDITOR.] The county auditor shall, within thirty days after the first school election held as provided herein, transmit to the State Auditor, to the Superintendent of Public Instruction and to the county superintendent, a plat of the county showing the boundaries and name of each school corporation therein, and shall record a copy of the same together with all proceedings of the county board had and done under this chapter in a proper book kept for that purpose. He shall promptly furnish such officers with a correct plat showing any changes at any time in the boundaries of school corporations. The Superintendent of Public Instruction shall furnish instructions for the suitable preparation and construction of such plats in regard to scale and markings, in order to secure a uniform series of maps for binding for office use.

## ARTICLE IV.

### ELECTION OF SCHOOL OFFICERS.

Section.
49. Officers to be Elected.
50. Polling Places, How Established—Appointment of Election Officers.
51. Who Qualified to Vote or Hold Office.
52. Hours Polls Open.
53. Notice of Annual Election.

Section.
54. Judges—Oath.
55. Election, How Conducted and Votes Canvassed.
56. Certificates of Election.
57. Oath of Office.

§ 49. (670.) OFFICERS TO BE ELECTED.] On the third Tuesday in June of each year there shall be elected one school director for the term of three years and on the third Tuesday in June of each even numbered year a school treasurer for the term of two years. Such officers shall hold their respective offices from the second Tuesday in July following their election for the number of years respectively for which they were elected, and until their successors are elected and qualified. At the first election for the organization of a new school district there shall be elected at large for such school districts three directors, one to serve until the first annual election, one to serve until the second annual election, and one to serve until the third annual election thereafter and a school treasurer to serve until the annual election in the next even numbered year and until his successor is elected and qualified.

§ 50. (671.) POLLING PLACES, HOW ESTABLISHED. APPOINT-
MENT OF ELECTION OFFICERS.] The county superintendent in
each county shall at least twenty days prior to the third Tuesday
in June of each year, fix and designate some polling place in
each school district so located as to be convenient for the voters
of such district, and shall appoint two persons to act as judges
and two to act as clerks of the election of such school officers;
such judges and clerks shall be qualified voters in their respective
districts. The county superintendent shall notify in writing such
judges and clerks of their appointment, and of the place fixed
and designated as the polling place in their respective districts,
and shall furnish them with the necessary blanks and poll books
for such election. He shall also furnish one of such clerks with
three notices of such election specifying the time and place at
which such election is to be held, the officers to be elected and
term of each, which notices such clerk shall post in three of the
most public places in the district at least ten days prior to the
thirteenth day of June. The county superintendent shall fix the
date and perform such other duties as devolve upon him by the
provisions of this section for the first election in any school
district hereafter formed under the provisions of this chapter,
and such election shall be called by the county superintendent
within thirty days after the formation of such school district.

§ 51. (672.) WHO QUALIFIED TO VOTE OR HOLD OFFICE.] At
any election of school officers in any school corporation in this
state, all persons who are qualified electors under the general
laws of the state and all women twenty-one years of age having
the necessary qualifications as to citizenship and residence
required of male voters by law, shall be qualified voters and shall
be eligible to the office of county superintendent of schools,
school director or member of the board of education or school
treasurer, or may be judge or clerk of such election.

§ 52. (673.) HOURS POLLS OPEN.] At all elections for school
district officers, the polls shall be open at 2 o'clock P. M. and
closed at 5 o'clock P. M.

§ 53. (674.) NOTICE OF ANNUAL ELECTION.] At least fifteen
days before the third Tuesday in June of each year the district
school board of each school district shall designate one polling
place as convenient as possible to the voters of such district at
which such annual election shall be held, and shall cause notice
of such election to be posted in at least three of the most public
and conspicuous places within the district. Such notices shall be
signed by the clerk or in his absence by the president of the
district school board, and shall state the time and place of holding such election and the officers to be elected and their term of
office, and shall be substantially in the following form:

Notice is hereby given that on Tuesday the ........ day of
June, A. D. ...... an election will be held at ............. (here
insert polling place) for the purpose of electing...............

(here insert officers to be elected and term each is to serve) for
school district No....... or for ........(here insert name of
school district). The polls will be open at 2 o'clock P. M. and
closed at 5 o'clock P. M. of that day.

By order of school board,

Signed, ..........................

Clerk.

§ 54. (675.) JUDGES. OATH.] At such annual election any
two of the directors of the school district may act as judges and
the clerk of the district school board and one other person to be
chosen by the voters present at the opening of the polls, shall
act as clerks. The voters present at the opening of the polls
shall choose a person to fill any vacancy caused by the absence
of either of such officers to act as judge or clerk of such election.
Before opening the polls each of the judges and clerks of election shall take and subscribe the following oath or affirmation:
"I do solemnly swear (or affirm) that I will perform my duties as
judge or clerk (as the case may be) according to law and the best
of my ability." Such oath or affirmation may be administered
by any officer authorized to administer oaths or by either of the
judges or clerks. Any school officer elected and qualified under
the provisions of this chapter is authorized and empowered to
administer any oath or affirmation pertaining in any manner to
school offices.

§ 55. (676.) ELECTION, HOW CONDUCTED AND VOTES CANVASSED.]
Such election shall be conducted and the votes canvassed as
provided by law for general elections, except as otherwise provided in this chapter. Immediately after the polls are closed the
judges shall proceed to count and canvass the votes for each
person voted for at such election for any office, and the person
receiving the highest number of votes for the office of director
or treasurer shall be declared elected. If the election results in
a tie for any such office, the district clerk shall immediately
notify in writing the parties having received such tie votes, and a
time shall be agreed upon by the parties within three days after
the election, at which the election shall be decided in the manner
that may be agreed upon by the parties, in the presence of the
judges and clerks of election, and a record of the proceedings
shall be made in the records of the district clerk. The return of
the number of votes cast for each person for county superintendent of schools, shall be signed by such judges and clerks of
election, sealed in an envelope and forwarded to the county
auditor within five days after such election.

§ 56. (677.) CERTIFICATES OF ELECTION.] The clerk of the
school district shall within five days after such election furnish
each person elected to any district office a written notice of his
election, and that he shall take the oath of office as such officer
on or before the second Tuesday in July following such election.
He shall also forward to the county superintendent within ten

days after such election, a certified list of all the officers elected thereat.

§ 57. (678.) OATH OF OFFICE.] Each person elected to the office of school director or treasurer shall before entering upon the duties of his office, take and subscribe the oath prescribed in section 211 of the constitution, which oath shall be filed with the clerk of the school district board.

## ARTICLE V.

### ORGANIZATION, MEETINGS AND DUTIES OF DISTRICT OFFICERS.

Section.
58. District School Board—Quorum.
59. Organization—Clerk.
60. Meetings of Board—Fees.
61. Duties of the President.
62. Duties of Clerk—Compensation.
63. Treasurer's Bond, How Approved—Vacancy how Filled.

Section.
64. When Additional Bonds Required.
65. School Funds, How Paid Out.
66. Warrants to be Indorsed When no Funds to Pay.
67. Warrants, What to Specify.
68. Oath and Bonds, Where to t . Filed.
69. Salary of School Treasurer.

§ 58. (679.) DISTRICT SCHOOL BOARD. QUORUM.] The three school directors in each school district shall constitute the district school board. A majority of the board shall constitute a quorum and the agreement of a majority shall be necessary to the validity of any contract entered into by the board.

§ 59. (680.) ORGANIZATION. CLERK.] The school board shall meet annually on the second Tuesday in July and organize by choosing one of the members president, and a competent person, not a member of the board, clerk, who shall hold his office during the pleasure of the board.

§ 60. (681.) MEETINGS OF BOARD. FEES.] The board shall on the second Tuesday in January, April, July and October of each year, hold regular meetings for the transaction of business at such hour and place as may be fixed by the board. A special meeting may be held upon the call of the president or of the other two members. Written notice of the time and place of any special meeting shall be given to each member of the board at least forty-eight hours before the time of such meeting. Each member of the board shall be paid the sum of eight dollars per annum, less two dollars for each regular meeting which he fails to attend.

§ 61. (682.) DUTIES OF THE PRESIDENT.] The president shall preside at all meetings of the board and shall perform such duties as usually pertain to such office and in accordance with the customary rules of order. In his absence a president *pro tempore* shall preside. The president shall perform such other duties as are prescribed in this chapter.

§ 62. (683.) DUTIES OF CLERK. COMPENSATION.] The clerk of the board shall keep an accurate record of all proceedings of the board, give or post all notices, make out all reports and statements and perform all other duties required by law or by the board. He shall receive such compensation as shall be fixed by the board, not less than five nor more than twenty-five dollars per annum.

§ 63. (684.) Treasurer's bond, how approved. Vacancy how filled.] The school treasurer shall, on or before the second Tuesday in July following his election and before entering upon his duties, give a bond to the school district conditioned for the honest and faithful discharge of his duties and that he will render a true account of all funds and property that shall come into his hands and pay and deliver the same according to law. Such bond shall be in such sum as may be fixed by the board, but not less than double the sum to come into his hands in any one year as nearly as may be ascertained, which bond shall be signed by two or more sufficient sureties to be approved by the school board. In case the school board neglects or refuses to approve the bond of such treasurer and the sureties thereon, such treasurer may present the same to the county superintendent and serve notice thereof upon the board and due proof of such notice being made to the county superintendent, he shall unless good cause for delay appears, proceed to hear and determime the sufficiency of the bond and the sureties thereon, and may approve or disapprove the same as the facts warrant. In case a vacancy occurs in the office of district treasurer, it shall be the duty of the county treasurer of the county wherein such school district is located, upon being notified by the county superintendent or clerk of such school district that such vacancy exists, to perform the duties of treasurer of such school district until the vacancy is duly filled.

§ 64. (685.) When additional bonds required.] Whenever the amount in the hands of the treasurer or subject to his order, exceeds two-thirds of the penal sum of his bond or when in the judgment of the board or of the county superintendent the security on such bond is impaired, the board or county superintendent shall require an additional bond. If the treasurer fails for twenty days to give such additional bond the office shall be declared vacant and the vacancy shall be filled as provided in this chapter.

§ 65. (686.) School funds, how paid out.] The school treasurer shall keep such accounts and make such reports as are required of him by law, and shall publish his annual statement in a newspaper published in the nearest city or town to his district. He shall pay no money out of the school funds in his hands except upon the warrant of the school board signed by the president and countersigned by the clerk. He shall pay all warrants properly drawn and signed when presented, if there is any money in his hands or subject to his order for their payment.

§ 66. (687.) Warrants to be indorsed when no funds to pay.] When a warrant is presented to the treasurer for payment and there is no money in his hands or subject to his order belonging to the proper fund for the payment of such warrant, he shall indorse on such warrant "presented for payment this.... day of............18..and not paid for want of funds," and shall sign such indorsement. If he has in his hands or subject to his order money for the part payment of such warrant, he shall make such part payment and indorse the sum on the warrant and add "balance not paid for want of funds," signing the same. He shall keep a correct register of all warrants so presented and indorsed. Each warrant thus presented and indorsed shall draw interest on the amount unpaid at eight per cent per annum from the date of such presentation and indorsement until paid; *provided*, that when there shall come into the hands of the treasurer or subject to his order money applicable to the payment of any warrant which has been so presented and registered, the treasurer shall notify in writing by mail the drawee of such warrant at his last known place of residence to present such warrant for payment, and interest shall cease upon every such warrant ten days after such notice shall have been sent, and such money shall be held for the payment of such warrant.

§ 67. (688.) WARRANTS, WHAT TO SPECIFY.] Each warrant drawn by the clerk of the board on the district treasurer must specify the purpose for which it is drawn, the fund on which it is drawn, and the person to whom payable; and no warrant shall be issued except for an indebtedness incurred prior to its issue.

§ 68. (689.) OATH AND BONDS, WHERE TO BE FILED.] All official oaths and bonds of school district officers shall be filed with the district clerk, who shall immediately certify to the county superintendent the fact of such oaths and bonds being filed. In case of the breach of any of the conditions of the treasurer's bond, the board, through its president, and in case of his refusal so to do, the county superintendent shall cause an action to be commenced and prosecuted thereon in the corporate name of the district, and any money collected for the district shall be paid to the district treasurer and any money collected for fines shall be paid into the county treasury and be credited to the general school fund of the state. If the board and county superintendent both fail or refuse to bring such action any taxpayer in the district may commence and prosecute such action, and the necessary expense thereof shall be paid out of the district treasury unless otherwise ordered by the court.

§ 69. (690.) SALARY OF SCHOOL TREASURER.] The school treasurer shall be paid for his services such sum as shall be fixed by the board not less than five nor more than twenty-five dollars per annum.

# ARTICLE VI.

## POWERS AND DUTIES OF DISTRICT SCHOOL BOARDS.

Section.
70. General Powers.
71. Power to Establish Schools.
72. Repairs, Fuel and Supplies.
73. Furniture, Maps, Registers, School Library.
74. Teachers, How Employed—Salaries, How Graded.
75. Pupils from Other Districts.
76. Rules—Suspension of Pupils.
77. Branches of Study.
78. Tax Levy—Notice to County Auditor.
79. When School Houses Can be Used for Other Purposes.

Section.
80. School Houses and Sites, How Determined.
81. *School House Sites, How Obtained.
82. Schools to be Organized on Petition.
83. School Terms, How Arranged—When Schools May be Discontinued.
84. Additional School Time.
85. District High Schools, How Established and Controlled.
86. School Census—Annual School Report.
87. Records Open to Inspection.
88. Records and Teaching in English.

§ 70. (691.) GENERAL POWERS.] The district school board shall have the general charge, direction and management of the schools of the district, and the care, custody and control of all the property belonging to it, subject to the provisions of this chapter.

§ 71. (692.) POWER TO ESTABLISH SCHOOLS.] It shall organize, maintain and conveniently locate schools for the education of children of school age within the district, and change or discontinue any of them in the cases provided by law.

§ 72. (693.) REPAIRS, FUEL AND SUPPLIES. It shall make all necessary repairs to the school houses, outbuildings and appurtenances, and shall furnish fuel and all necessary supplies for the schools.

§ 73. (694.) FURNITURE, MAPS, REGISTERS, SCHOOL LIBRARY.] It shall furnish to each school all necessary and suitable furniture, maps, charts and apparatus, including Webster's International Dictionary. The school registers and all school blanks used shall be those furnished by the State Department of Public Instruction. It shall have power to purchase and keep for the use of the inhabitants of the school district a circulating library of the value of not more than fifty dollars, to be selected by the school board from any list of books approved by the Superintendent of Public Instruction, and furnished to the county superintendents for that purpose, and it shall not purchase any books not contained in such list. With the consent of a majority of the voters of the district at a meeting duly called for that purpose, due notice of which has been given as·provided by law for other meetings of the voters of the school district, the district school board may purchase and select a library of the value of more than fifty dollars but not to exceed one hundred dollars in value. It shall have the care and custody of the library and may appoint as librarian any suitable person including one of their own number. It shall make rules to govern the circulation and care of the books while in the hands of pupils or other persons and may impose and collect penalties for injuries done to any book by the act, negligence or permission of the person who takes the same or while in his possession. No book shall be loaned for a longer period than two weeks at any time to any one person and never to any person not a resident of the district. The library shall be open at least once each week for the accommodation of its patrons. It shall, under proper rules, permit teachers to take books from the library to their schools for use in illustrating any subject and for instruction. It may at any time exchange any part or all of its library with any other district or person, so far as different books may be so obtained, for equal values of the books exchanged, and may at any time accept donations of books for the library; but it shall exclude therefrom all books unsuited to the cultivation of good character and good morals and manners, and no sectarian publications devoted to the discussion of sectarian differencies and creeds shall be admitted to the library.

§ 74. (695.) TEACHERS, HOW EMPLOYED. SALARIES, HOW GRADED.] It shall employ the teachers of the school district, and may dismiss a teacher at any time for plain violation of contract, gross immorality or flagrant neglect of duty.' No person shall be permitted to teach in any public school who is not the holder of a teacher's certificate or a permit to teach, valid in the county or district in which such school is situated; and every contract for the employment of a teacher must be in writing, and such contract must be executed before such teacher begins to teach in such schools. It shall grade the salaries of teachers for the district in accordance with the grades of certificates, and no teacher holding a certificate of a lower grade shall be paid a salary equal to or in excess of that paid to a teacher holding a certificate of a higher grade in the same district.

§ 75. (696.) PUPILS FROM OTHER DISTRICTS.] It shall have power to admit to the schools in the district, pupils from other districts when it can be done without injuring or overcrowding such schools, and shall make regulations for their admission and the payment of their tuition. It shall have power to arrange with the board of an adjacent district for sending to such district such pupils as can be conveniently taught therein, and for paying their tuition. It shall also have power to make proper and needful rules for the assignment and distribution of pupils to and among the schools in the district and their transfer from one school to another.

§ 76. (697.) RULES. SUSPENSION OF PUPILS.] It shall assist and co-operate with teachers in the government and discipline of the schools, and may make proper rules and regulations therefor. It may suspend or expel from school any pupil who is insubordinate or habitually disobedient, but such suspension shall not be for a longer period than ten days nor such expulsion beyond the end of the current term of school.

§ 77. (698.) BRANCHES OF STUDY.] Subject to the approval of the county superintendent, it shall have power to determine

S. L.—4.

what branches, if any, in addition to those required by law shall be taught in any school of the district.     •

§ 78. (699.) TAX LEVY. NOTICE TO COUNTY AUDITOR.] It shall have power to levy upon the property in the district a tax for school purposes of not exceeding thirty mills on the dollar in any year, which levy shall be made by resolution of the board prior to the twentieth day of July. The clerk shall immediately thereafter notify in writing the county auditor of the amount of tax so levied. It shall not have power to abate or reduce the amount of tax so levied after the county auditor has been notified of the amount of such levy.

§ 79. (700.) WHEN SCHOOL HOUSES CAN BE USED FOR OTHER PURPOSES.] It may permit a school house, when not occupied for school purposes, to be used under careful restrictions for any proper purpose, giving equal rights and privileges to all religious denominations or political parties, but for any such use or privilege it shall not be at any cost for fuel or otherwise to the district. Nor shall any furniture which is fastened to the floor be removed, and whoever removes any school furniture for any other purpose than repairing the same or for repairing the school room shall be guilty of a misdemeanor and shall be fined not less than five nor more than ten dollars for each offense. All fines imposed and collected under the provisions of this section shall be paid into the general school fund of the State.

§ 80. (701.) SCHOOL HOUSES AND SITES, HOW DETERMINED.] Whenever in the judgment of the board it is desirable or necessary to the welfare of the schools in the district or to provide for the children therein proper school privileges, or whenever petitioned so to do by one-third of the voters in the district, the board shall call a meeting of the voters in the district at some convenient time and place fixed by the board to vote upon the question of the selection, purchase, exchange or sale of a school house site, or the erection, removal or sale of a school house. The president of the board shall be the chairman and the clerk of the board, secretary of such meeting. In case either of these officers is not present, his place shall be filled by some one chosen by the voters present. Three notices of the time, place and purpose of such meeting shall be posted in three public places in the district by the clerk, at least ten days prior to such meeting. If a majority of the voters present at such meeting shall by vote select a school house site, or shall be in favor of the purchase, exchange or sale of the school house, as the case may be, the board shall locate, purchase, exchange or sell such site, or erect, remove or sell such school house, as the case may be, in accordance with such vote; *provided*, that it shall require a vote of two-thirds of the voters present and voting at such meeting to order the removal of the school house and such school house so removed cannot again be removed within three years from the date of such meeting.

§ 81. (702.) SCHOOL HOUSE SITES, HOW OBTAINED.] The school board of any school district may take in the corporate name thereof, any real property not exceeding two acres in area chosen as a site for school house, as provided in this chapter, and may hold and use such tract for school purposes only. Should the owner of such real property refuse or neglect to grant and convey such site, a site for such school house may be obtained by proceeding in eminent domain as provided in the code of civil procedure. If the sight so selected is not used for the purposes for which it is taken for two successive years, it shall revert to the original owner or his assigns upon repayment of the sum originally paid by the corporation together with a reasonable consideration for the improvement. If such owner or his assigns neglects or refuses to make such repayment for one year after demand therefor by the board such site shall be the property of the district.

§ 82. (703.) SCHOOLS TO BE ORGANIZED ON PETITION.] If a petition signed by the persons charged with the support and having the custody and care of nine or more children of school age, all of whom reside not less than two and one-half miles from the nearest school is presented to the board asking for the organization of a school for such children, the board shall organize such school and employ a teacher therefor if a suitable room for such school can be leased or rented at some proper location, not more than two and one-half miles distant from the residence of any one of such children, and if such petition is signed by the persons charged with the support and having the custody and care of twelve or more of such children the board shall organize a school and employ a teacher therefor, and if no suitable room for such school can be leased or rented, the board shall call a meeting of the voters of the district for the selection and purchase of a school house site therefor and the purchase or erection of a school house as provided for in section 700. If at such meeting no such site is selected or if it is not voted to erect or purchase a school house for such school the board shall select and purchase a school house site, and erect, purchase or move thereon a school house at a cost of not more than seven hundred dollars for such house and furniture therefor.

§ 83. (704.) SCHOOL TERMS, HOW ARRANGED. WHEN SCHOOLS MAY BE DISCONTINUED.] The district board shall determine and fix the length of time the schools of the district shall be taught in each year, and when each term of school shall begin and end. It shall so arrange such terms as to accommodate and furnish school privileges equally and equitably to pupils of all ages; *provided*, that every common school shall be kept in session for at least four months in each school year, and in each district in which the number of persons of school age is an average of fifteen or more to the school, each school shall be kept in session for at least six months in each school year; *provided, further*, that

any school may be discontinued when the number of pupils of
school age residing nearest to such school shall be less than four,
and all contracts between school boards and teachers shall
contain a provision that no compensation shall be received by
such teacher from the date of such discontinuance or when with
the consent of a majority of the patrons of such school proper
and convenient school facilities can be provided for the pupils
therein in some other school.

§ 84. (705.) ADDITIONAL SCHOOL TIME.] If a majority of
the patrons of any school averaging for its last term twelve or
more pupils in daily attendance, shall petition the board to
continue such school for an additional time, not exceeding nine
months in any school year, the board shall continue such school
for that length of time, if there are funds in the treasury sufficient
for that purpose.

§ 85. (706.) DISTRICT HIGH SCHOOLS, HOW ESTABLISHED AND
CONTROLLED.] In any district containing four or more common
schools and having an enumeration of sixty or more persons of
school age residing therein the board may call, and if petitioned
so to do by ten or more voters in the district, shall call a meeting
of the voters of such district in the manner prescribed in section
700 to determine the question of the establishment of a district
high school. If a majority of the voters at such meeting vote in
favor of establishing such high school, the meeting shall further
proceed to select a site therefor and to provide for the erection
or purchase of a school building, or for the necessary addition to
some school building therefor. Thereupon the board shall erect
or purchase a building or make such addition for such high
school, as shall be determined at such meeting, and shall establish therein a district high school containing one or more
departments, and employ teachers therefor. Such school shall
be kept in session for such time each year not less than three
months, as the board may determine. The board shall, subject
to the approval of the county superintendent, grade such high
school and prescribe the studies to be pursued therein, and shall
have the same management and control thereof as of the common
schools in the district. Two or more adjacent school districts
may join in the establishment and maintenance of such high
school, when empowered so to do by a majority of the voters in
each district at a meeting called and held as provided for in this
section, in which case the building and furniture occupied and
used for such high school shall belong to the districts so uniting,
and all the costs of maintaining such school, including wages of
teachers and all necessary supplies shall be paid by such districts
in proportion to the assessed valuation of the property in each,
and the employment of teachers therefor, and the management,
control and grading thereof shall be vested in the joint boards of
such districts, subject to the approval of the county superintendent of the county in which such school is situated.

§ 86. (707.) SCHOOL CENSUS. ANNUAL SCHOOL REPORT.] The board shall cause the clerk to make an enumeration each year of all unmarried persons of school age, being over six and under twenty years of age, having their legal residence in the district on the first day of December of that year, giving the name and age of such persons and the name of the parent or guardian having the care or custody of each. Such enumeration shall be made upon and in accordance with the blanks furnished therefor by the county superintendent and shall be returned to the county superintendent prior to the twentieth day of December. A copy of such enumeration shall also be kept in the office of the district clerk. The board shall also cause the district clerk to make out an annual school report for the year beginning January first and ending December thirty-first, containing such financial and statistical statements and items as shall be required by the Superintendent of Public Instruction upon and in accordance with the blanks furnished therefor by the county superintendent. Such report shall be carefully examined and certified as correct by the board at its regular meeting in January and transmitted to the county superintendent prior to the first day of February following. A copy of such report shall be filed in the district clerk's office.

§ 87. (708.) RECORDS OPEN TO INSPECTION.] All reports, books, records, vouchers, contracts, and papers relating to school business in a school district in the office of the clerk or treasurer, shall at all times be open to the inspection of any director, who shall advise and aid in securing correct records and accounts and legal reports, and they shall likewise be open to the Superintendent of Public Instruction, and county superintendent and any particular paper or record shall be exhibited at reasonable hours to any voter or tax payer.

§ 88. (709.) RECORDS AND TEACHING IN ENGLISH.] All reports and records of school officers and proceedings of all school meetings shall be in the English language, and if any money belonging to any district shall be expended in supporting a school in which the English language shall not be taught exclusively, the county superintendent or any taxpayer of the school corporation may in a civil action in the name of the corporation recover for such corporation all such money from the officer so expending it or ordering or voting for its expenditure.

# ARTICLE VII.

## SCHOOL FUNDS.

Section.
89. State Tuition Fund, How Raised.
90. County Treasurer to Report Funds Quarterly—State Superintendent Apportions.
91. Funds Defined—How Used.
92. Funds Controlled and Paid Out by District Treasurer.
93. Not Entitled to Tuition Fund, When—Enumeration.
94. Apportionment of Funds by County Superintendent.

Section.
95. Special Districts Entitled to Tuition Fund.
96. Treasurer's Accounts—Annual Settlement.
97. When County Treasurer to Pay Funds to District Treasurer.
98. County Treasurer to Keep Accounts with School Corporations.
99. School Taxes, How and When Collected.

§ 89. (710.) STATE TUITION FUND, HOW RAISED.] The net proceeds arising from all fines and penalties for violation of state laws, from leasing the school lands, the interest and income from the state permanent school fund together with the school poll tax and all school taxes levied by a general law shall be collected and paid into the state treasury in the same manner as is provided by law for the collection and payment of state taxes, and shall constitute the state tuition fund, which shall be apportioned among the several counties of the state in proportion to the number of children of school age in each, as shown by the last enumeration authorized by law.

§ 90. (711.) COUNTY TREASURER TO REPORT FUNDS QUARTERLY. STATE SUPERINTENDENT APPORTIONS.] It shall be the duty of the county treasurer to receive from the proper officers the net proceeds of fines, penalties and forfeitures for violation of state laws, to collect the school poll tax and all taxes levied for school purposes by general law, and all moneys arising from leasing school lands within the county, and to forward a detailed statement of the moneys so collected, specifying the amount received from each of the above sources, to the state auditor at the same time that he is required to make reports of other moneys to such auditor. It shall be the duty of the State Auditor on or before the third Monday in February, May, August and November in each year to certify to the Superintendent of Public Instruction the amount of the state tuition fund and the State Superintendent shall immediately apportion such fund among the several counties of the state in proportion to the number of children of school age residing in each as shown by the last enumeration provided for by law, and certify to the State Auditor, State Treasurer and to the county treasurer and county superintendent of each county, the amount apportioned to the respective counties. Immediately upon receipt of such apportionment from the State Superintendent as herein provided, the State Auditor shall draw a warrant upon the State Treasurer for the full amount of the State Tuition Fund apportioned to the several counties and shall deliver the same to the State Treasurer taking his receipt therefor, and shall notify the several county treasurers of the amount due their respective counties and that such warrant has been issued therefor and the State Treasurer shall pay on such warrant to the several county treasurers the amount due their respective counties; *provided, however*, that all moneys arising from interest on the permanent school fund and from leasing school lands shall be apportioned under a separate item and such money shall be taken account of as a separate item by all officers making or certifying such apportionment, or through whose hands any portion of such fund shall pass and it is further made the duty of the district treasurer to keep such fund separate from all other funds and if at the close of the school year any part of such fund which was apportioned prior to the third Monday of November of such year remains in the hands of the district treasurer, he shall return the same to the county treasurer taking his receipt therefor, and the county treasurer shall return all such funds so returned or that were not drawn by the district treasurer from the county treasurer to the State Treasurer who shall receipt for the same, and the county treasurer shall certify to the State Auditor the amount so returned to the State Treasurer.

§ 91. (712.) FUNDS DEFINED. HOW USED.] All money received by the school district from the apportionment made by the Superintendent of Public Instruction shall constitute and be designated the State Tuition Fund. All money received from district taxes, from subscription, from sale of property, or from any other source whatever except from apportionment made by the Superintendent of Public Instruction, shall be designated the special fund. In addition to the State Tuition Fund and the special fund, a sinking fund may be established as provided by this article. The State Tuition Fund shall be used only in the payment of teachers' wages; *provided*, that if the State Tuition Fund apportioned to any district in any one year is insufficient for the payment of teachers' wages in such district any money on hand or available belonging to the special fund of such district may be applied to meet such deficiency; *provided, further*, that if the State Tuition Fund apportioned to any one district in any one year is more than sufficient for the payment of teachers' wages in such district the portion of such fund in excess of the amount so required may be applied to the payment of warrants drawn upon the special fund of such district, if such district has school the required number of months during such year as required by law.

§ 92. (713.) FUNDS CONTROLLED AND PAID OUT BY DISTRICT TREASURER.] All funds shall be kept in the possession or under the control of and paid out by the district treasurer, and he shall keep one general account for each district of the entire receipts and expenditures, and separate itemized accounts as herein provided for each class of receipts and expenditures. His books shall at all times show by entries under proper heads all receipts of funds and payments therefrom, so as to enable any person readily to ascertain any balance in any account or any funds.

§ 93. (714.) Not entitled to tuition fund, when. Enumeration.] No school district shall be entitled to receive any
portion of the State Tuition Fund that fails to make a report of
the enumeration of children of school age in the manner provided by law, nor until such enumeration has been taken and
reported as required by law. The county superintendent of
schools shall not authorize the payment of money apportioned
to any district unless the bond and oath of such treasurer duly
approved and certified are on file in the office of the district clerk
and a certificate thereof filed in the office of the county superintendent. New districts organized after the annual enumeration
has been taken shall proceed immediately to take the enumeration as provided by law, and after the receipt of such enumeration
by the Superintendent of Public Instruction through the county
superintendent, the newly organized districts shall receive their
proportionate share of the funds to be apportioned.

§ 94. (715.) Apportionment of funds by county superintendent.] Within thirty days and in not less than twenty days
after receiving the certificate of apportionment from the Superintendent of Public Instruction the county superintendent shall
apportion separately to the several school districts, special
districts and districts organized under special law, which are
entitled to any portion of the State Tuition Fund within the
county in proportion to the number of children residing in each
over six and under twenty years of age, excluding all married
persons, as appears from the last enumeration authorized by law
upon which the Superintendent of Public Instruction made the
apportionment to the several counties, and he shall immediately
notify each district treasurer of the amount of money due his
school district, and shall certify to the county treasurer and to
the county auditor the amount due each school district. The
county treasurer shall deliver to the several district treasurers
upon the order of the county auditor the amounts apportioned to
their respective districts, taking a receipt therefor.

§ 95. (716.) Special districts entitled to tuition fund.]
Special school districts shall be entitled to receive their proportion
of the State Tuition Fund; provided that the clerk or secretary of
the board of education thereof shall make a report to the county
superintendent of the enumeration of children of school age
therein at the time and in the manner prescribed in this chapter
for other school districts to report the same.

§ 96. (717.) Treasurer's accounts. Annual settlement.]
The district treasurer shall open new accounts with each fund at
the beginning of each school year and the balance in each fund
shall be brought down and become the first entry in opening the
account for the new year. On the Tuesday in January succeeding
the annual meeting of the school board in each year, the school
board shall make settlement with the district treasurer and shall
carefully examine his books, accounts and vouchers and shall

ascertain if the amount of all warrants, bonds and coupons paid and redeemed or paid in part together with the cash in his hands or under his control, is equal to the amount of the cash on hand at the beginning of the school year, together with all money received by him from all sources for school purposes during the year. The district treasurer shall deliver to the board at such annual meeting all warrants, bonds and coupons paid and redeemed by him during the school year and held by him as vouchers taking the receipt of the board therefor, and such vouchers shall forthwith be filed with the district clerk. He shall at that meeting make his annual report in triplicate, one copy to be preserved in the treasurer's office, one to be filed with the clerk of the school board, and one to be transmitted to the county superintendent of schools, and the board shall cause to be published an itemized statement of the receipts and expenditures of the preceding year. The treasurer's reports shall show the following:

### RECEIPTS.

The balance at the close of the year.
The amount received into the State Tuition Fund.
The amount received into the Special Fund.
The amount received into the Sinking Fund.

### EXPENDITURES.

The amount paid for school houses, sites and furniture.
The amount paid for apparatus and fixtures.
The amount paid for teachers' wages.
The amount paid for services and expenses of school officers.
The amount paid for redemption of bonds.
The amount paid for interest on bonds.
The amount paid for incidental expenses.
The cash on hand at the close of the school year.

Such report shall include such other items as may be required by the district board or the Superintendent of Public Instruction, and shall be upon and in conformity with the blanks furnished him for that purpose.

§ 97. (718.) WHEN COUNTY TREASURER TO PAY FUNDS TO DISTRICT TREASURER.] The treasurer of each district shall apply to the county auditor for an order, and the county treasurer, shall pay over to him on such order all of the school money collected for such district and all school money apportioned to such district by the county superintendent, and the county auditor shall issue such order when notified by the county superintendent in writing that such district treasurer has qualified and filed his oath and bond as provided by law. But no such notice of qualification is required during the term of each district treasurer, and when a new one is appointed for any reason or the incumbent has become disqualified, the clerk of the school board shall so inform the county superintendent, who shall also inform the county auditor. It shall be the duty of the county treasurer when payment is made to any school treasurer of any funds herein provided for, immediately to notify the clerk of the school board of the payment of the same.

§ 98. (719.) COUNTY TREASURER TO KEEP ACCOUNTS WITH SCHOOL CORPORATIONS.] Each county treasurer shall keep a regular account with each school corporation, in which he shall charge himself with all taxes collected by levy of the district school board and all sums apportioned to the district by the county superintendent or other authority, and all sums received for the district, and he shall credit himself with all payments made to the treasurer of the district, distinguishing between the items paid by apportionment, those from local taxes, and those from other sources. He shall also credit himself with all payments for redemption or indorsement of warrants in the collection of taxes and shall deliver to the district treasurer a duplicate tax receipt for the amount of each warrant so indorsed or redeemed together with all warrants so redeemed, at the time of making other regular payments to the district treasurer. To these credits, to balance the accounts, he shall add all items for legal fees, for collection and other duties.

§ 99. (720.) SCHOOL TAXES, HOW AND WHEN COLLECTED.] It shall be the duty of the county treasurer to collect the taxes for school purposes at the same time and in the same manner that the county and State taxes are collected, and full power is hereby given to him to sell property for school taxes the same as is provided by law for the collection of other taxes. Whenever an error occurs in any school corporation's tax list the district school board or board of education in special districts may correct such errors and refund such taxes improperly collected. All penalties and interest collected on delinquent school taxes shall be applied to the proper fund to which such delinquent taxes belong.

## ARTICLE VIII.

### TAXES.

Section.
100. School Board to Levy Tax.
101. Tax, How Levied.
102. Maximum Levy for Final Judgment—Taxes to be Uniform.

Section.
103. Statement of Assessed Valuation.
104. Indebtedness of District, How Adjusted When Board Illegal or Failure to Elect.

§ 100. (721.) SCHOOL BOARD TO LEVY TAX.] Each district school board shall have power and it shall be its duty to levy upon all the property subject to taxation in the district a tax for school purposes of all kinds authorized by law, not exceeding in the aggregate a rate of thirty mills on the dollar in any one year.

Such tax shall be levied by resolution of the board prior to the twentieth day of July in each year, which resolution shall be entered in the records of the proceedings of the board. The clerk shall immediately thereafter notify the county auditor in writing of the amount of tax so levied, and such notice shall be in substantially the following form:

State of North Dakota,    &#125;
County of .................... &#125; ss.
........School District........ &#125;
To...............................
     County Auditor of ....................County.
Sir:
    You are hereby notified that the school board of ............ school district has levied a tax of .........dollars upon all real and personal property in said school district for school purposes. You will duly enter and extend such tax upon the county tax list for collection, upon the taxable property of such school district for the current year.
    Dated at.........this....day of ........189..
    .................................
                        District Clerk.

The notice of a tax to pay any judgment against the district shall be in addition to the regular tax and shall be certified to the county auditor under the same general form, as near as may be; *provided*, that if the boundaries of such district shall embrace a portion of two counties then the clerk of such district shall certify to the county auditor of the county in which is located the original district to which such portion of the district embraced in the other county is attached, in addition to the tax levy above mentioned, a list and valuation of all property subject to taxation in such portion of such district embraced in the other county, as shown by the assessor making the assessment in such county, township or assessor's district, and the auditor shall enter such property upon the tax duplicate of his county and levy all school taxes upon the same, and the county treasurer of the county shall collect the taxes levied thereon the same as other taxes are collected and pay the same over to the treasurer of the district entitled thereto.

§ 101. (722.) TAX, HOW LEVIED.] The county auditor of each county shall at the time of making the annual assessment and levy of taxes, levy a tax of one dollar on each elector in the county for the support of common schools, and a further tax of two mills on the dollar upon all the taxable property in the county, to be collected at the same time and in the same manner as other taxes are collected, which shall be apportioned by the county superintendent of schools among the school districts of the county as provided by law.

§ 102. (723.) MAXIMUM LEVY FOR FINAL JUDGMENT. TAXES TO BE UNIFORM.] When any final judgment shall be obtained against a school district the board thereof shall levy a tax upon the taxable property of such district not exceeding in amount twenty mills on the dollar in any one year, which shall be used in the payment thereof. The county auditor shall make out, charge and extend upon the tax list against each description of real property and against all personal property, and upon all taxable property of the district, all such taxes for schools and judgments he is so notified has been levied by the district in which the property is situated and taxable, in the same manner in which the county and State tax list is prepared, and deliver it to the county treasurer at the same time. All taxes for school purposes shall be uniform upon the property within each school district.

§ 103. (724.) STATEMENT OF ASSESSED VALUATION.] Each assessor shall on or before the first day of July in each year furnish to the clerk of the school district, to the county superintendent of schools and to the county auditor a statement of the assessed valuation of all the property in such corporation subject to taxation.

§ 104. (725.) INDEBTEDNESS OF DISTRICT, HOW ADJUSTED WHEN BOARD ILLEGAL OR FAILURE TO ELECT.] If any school district in the State has for one or more years past, either through failure to elect a school board or through failure of the county superintendent to appoint a school board, been without a legal school board or if hereafter any school district through such failure to elect or to appoint such school board shall be without such legal school board, and such district shall have an authorized indebtedness either in bonds, interest due on bonds or otherwise, it shall be the duty of the county superintendent, the county treasurer and county auditor, acting as a board of adjusters, to assess upon the taxable property of such school corporation a tax not to exceed twenty mills on the dollar in any one year upon the assessed valuation thereof for the payment of the same. Which tax so levied shall be extended upon the tax lists by the county auditor and be collected by the county treasurer as other taxes are collected and shall be applied upon and used for the payment of such indebtedness, and shall be paid to the creditors of such district upon the warrant of the county auditor countersigned by the county superintendent, and all warrants, bonds, interest coupons, receipted bills or accounts shall be filed in the office of the county auditor and in case such school corporation has a bonded indebtedness, it shall be the duty of such board of adjusters to levy a tax upon the property of such district sufficient to create a sinking fund for the redemption of such bonds upon the maturity of the same, such sinking fund to be levied and provided for in compliance with the requirements of such bonds.

# ARTICLE IX.

## VACANCIES.

Section.
105. Vacancy in Office of Superintendent Public Instruction Filled by Appointment.
106. Vacancy in Office of County Superintendent, How Filled.

Section.
107. Vacancy in Office of Director or Treasurer, How Filled.
108. Vacancy in Office of Clerk, How Filled.
109. Office, When Deemed Vacant.

§ 105. (726.) Vacancy in office superintendent public instruction filled by appointment.] Should a vacancy occur in the office of the Superintendent of Public Instruction, the Governor shall have power and it shall be his duty to fill such vacancy by appointment, which appointment shall be valid until the next general election and until his successor is elected and qualified.

§ 106. (727.) Vacancy in office of county superintendent, how filled.] Should a vacancy occur in the office of county superintendent of schools, the board of county commissioners of such county shall have power and it shall be their duty to fill such vacancy by appointment, as provided by law, which appointment shall be valid until the next annual school election. The county auditor shall immediately notify the Superintendent of Public Instruction of such appointment.

§ 107. (728.) Vacancy in office of director or treasurer, how filled.] When any vacancy occurs in the office of director or treasurer of a school district by death, resignation, removal from the district, or otherwise, the fact of such vacancy shall be immediately certified to the county superintendent by the clerk of the district, and such superintendent shall immediately appoint in writing some competent person, who shall qualify and serve until the next annual school election. The county superintendent shall at the same time notify the clerk of the school district and the county auditor of every such appointment.

§ 108. (729.) Vacancy in office of clerk, how filled.] Should the office of clerk of a school district become vacant, the school board shall immediately fill such vacancy by appointment and the president of the board shall immediately notify the county superintendent and the county auditor of such appointment.

§ 109. (730.) Office, when deemed vacant.] Any office of a school district shall become vacant by resignation of the incumbent thereof, but such resignation shall not take effect until a successor has qualified according to law. Any office of a school district shall be deemed vacant if the person duly elected thereto shall neglect or refuse for the period of two weeks after the beginning of the term for which he was elected, to accept and qualify for such office and serve therein. Any school officer may be removed from office by a court of competent jurisdiction, as provided by law.

# ARTICLE X.

## EQUALIZATION OF INDEBTEDNESS.

Section.
110. Equalization of Indebtedness, by Arbitration.
111. Tax to Equalize and Pay Previous Debts.
112. Maximum Annual Tax Levy for Such Purposes.

Section.
113. Proceeds to be Turned Over to the Respective Districts.
114. Maximum Tax Levy for all School Purposes.

§ 110. (731.) EQUALIZATION OF INDEBTEDNESS, BY ARBITRATION.] After the boundaries of a school district have been established as provided for in this chapter, all school districts or parts of school districts that existed as school corporations before the taking effect of this code and that are now included in one school district shall effect an equalization of property, funds on hand and debts. To effect this each school board of such corporation, constituting a school district under the operation of this chapter, shall select one arbitrator and the several arbitrators so selected together with the county superintendent shall constitute a board of arbitration to effect such equalization. If in any case the number of abitrators, including the county superintendent shall be an even number, the county treasurer shall be included and be a member of such board. The county superintendent shall fix the time and place of such meeting.

§ 111. (732.) TAX TO EQUALIZE AND PAY PREVIOUS DEBTS.] Such board shall take an account of the assets, funds on hand, the debts properly and justly belonging to or chargeable to each corporation or part of a corporation as it or they existed heretofore, and levy such a tax against each as will in its judgment justly and fairly equalize their several interests.

§ 112. (733.) MAXIMUM ANNUAL TAX LEVY FOR SUCH PURPOSES.] When the amounts to be levied upon the several corporations or parts of corporations mentioned in the preceding section shall be fixed, a list thereof shall be made wherein the amount shall be set down opposite each corporation. The whole shall be stated substantially in the form herein required for certifying school taxes and addressed to the county auditor, and shall be signed by a majority of such board of arbitration; such levy shall be deemed' legal and valid upon the taxable property of each corporation; *provided, however,* that not more than fifteen mills thereof shall be extended against such taxable property in any one year, and such a levy not exceeding fifteen mills on the dollar shall be extended as in this section provided, from year to year, until the whole amount shall be so levied. The county auditor shall preserve such levies and shall extend the several rates from year to year, as above required by law for district taxes and the taxes shall be collected at the same time and in the same manner as other taxes are collected.

§ 113. (734.) PROCEEDS TO BE TURNED OVER TO THE RESPECTIVE DISTRICTS.] Opposite the several descriptions of property on the tax list shall be entered the school district within which it lies, and all the proceeds of these equalizing taxes shall be collected and paid over to the treasurer of the proper school district within which the property is situated. The proceeds of taxes upon parts of districts lying outside of the districts as at present constituted, with which they were equalized, shall be paid to the treasurer of the school district within which the property is situated, the same as hereinbefore provided for regular taxes.

§ 114. (735.) MAXIMUM TAX LEVY FOR ALL SCHOOL PURPOSES.] The taxes levied for purposes of equalization shall be in addition to all other taxes for school purposes; *provided*, that all taxes for school purposes, including such taxes for equalization, shall not exceed thirty mills on the dollar in any one year. The provisions of this article shall apply to and govern all school districts and parts of school districts hereafter divided or consolidated with each other, or with other districts in the division uniting or apportionment of their debts and liabilities or property and assets.

## ARTICLE XI.

### EXAMINATIONS AND CERTIFICATES.

Section.
115. Examinations for Teachers' Certificates.
116. Professional Certificates, Who Entitled.
117. Normal Certificates, Who Entitled.
118. Fee for Certificate—Certificate, How Revoked.
119. Examination of Teachers by County Superintendent.
120. Teachers Grades, How Established—Reexaminations, When Allowed.

Section.
121. Qualifications of Teachers—Contracts, When Void.
122. Fee for Certificate.
123. Certificates, When Revocable.
124. Proceedings to Revoke—Teachers Allowed Defense.

§ 115. (736.) EXAMINATIONS FOR TEACHERS' CERTIFICATES.] The Superintendent of Public Instruction shall prepare or cause to be prepared all questions for the examination of applicants for teachers' certificates both county and State, and shall prescribe rules for the conduct of all such examinations.

§ 116. (737.) PROFESSIONAL CERTIFICATES, WHO ENTITLED.] He may issue a State certificate to be valid for life, unless sooner revoked, to be known as a professional certificate. Such certificate shall be issued only to those persons of good moral character, who pass a thorough examination in all the branches included in the courses of study prescribed for the common and high schools of the State, including methods of teaching and such other branches as the Superintendent of Public Instruction may direct. Such certificates shall in no case be granted unless the applicant has had an experience as a teacher of at least five years, and can satisfy such superintendent of his ability to instruct and properly manage any high school of the State. Such certificate shall be valid throughout the State and the holder shall be authorized to teach in any of the common or high schools of the State without further examination; *provided,* that any person who is a graduate of the four years' normal course in the University of North Dakota, and has had three years successful experience as a teacher, may be granted such professional certificate without further examination; *provided, further,* that if the holder of a professional certificate shall at any time cease to teach, or to be engaged in other active educational work for the space of three years, he shall be liable to a re-examination and to the cancellation of his certificate, subject to such rules as may be prescribed by such superintendent.

§ 117. (738.) NORMAL CERTIFICATE, WHO ENTITLED.] He may issue a State certificate, to be valid for a term of five years, unless sooner revoked, to be known as a normal certificate. Such certificate shall be issued only to those persons of good moral character who have completed the prescribed course of study in one of the normal schools of the state or in a normal school elsewhere having an established reputation for thoroughness, but the Superintendent of Public Instruction may examine any such applicant in his discretion. Such certificate shall not be granted unless the applicant shall have taught school successfully for at least two years. Such certificate shall be valid throughout the State and the holder shall be authorized to teach in any of the public schools of the state; *provided,* that any person who is a graduate of the four years' normal course in the University of North Dakota, and who has had one year's successful experience as a teacher, may be granted such normal certificate without further examination. No State certificate shall hereafter be issued by any normal school in the State.

§ 118. (739.) FEE FOR CERTIFICATE. CERTIFICATE, HOW REVOKED.] The superintendent shall require a fee of five dollars from each applicant for a professional or normal certificate, which fee shall be used by him to aid in the establishment and maintenance of Teachers' Reading Circles in the State. He shall revoke at any time any certificate issued in the State, for any cause which would have been sufficient ground for refusing to issue the same had the cause existed or been known at the time it was issued.

§ 119. (740.) EXAMINATION OF TEACHERS BY COUNTY SUPERINTENDENT.] The county superintendent shall hold a public examination of all persons over eighteen years of age, offering themselves as candidates for teachers of common schools at the most suitable place in the county, on the second Friday in January, March, May, July, September and November of each year, and, when necessary, such examination may be continued on the following day, at which times he shall examine them by a series of written or printed questions, according to the rules prescribed by the Superintendent of Public Instruction. If from the percentage of correct answers required by the rules and other evidence disclosed by the examination, including particularly the superintendent's knowledge and information of the candidate's successful experience, if any, the applicant is found to be a person of good moral character, to possess a knowledge and understanding together with aptness to teach and govern, which will enable such applicant to teach in the common schools of the State the various branches required by law, such superintendent shall grant to such applicant a certificate of qualification.

§ 120. (741.) TEACHERS' GRADES, HOW ESTABLISHED. RE-EXAMINATION, WHEN ALLOWED.] Such certificates shall be of three regular grades, the first grade for a term of three years, the second grade for a term of two years, and the third grade for one year, according to the ratio of correct answers of each applicant and other evidence of qualification appearing from the examination. No certificate shall be granted unless the applicant shall be found proficient in and qualified to teach the following branches of a common English education: Reading, writing, orthography, language lessons and English grammar, geography, United States history, arithmetic, civil government, physiology and hygiene, and for a first and second grade can pass a satisfactory examination in theory and practice of teaching. In addition to the above, applicants for a first grade certificate shall pass a satisfactory examination in physical geography, elements of natural philosophy, elements of physiology, elementary geometry and algebra. The percentage required to pass any branch shall be prescribed by the Superintendent of Public Instruction. In addition to these regular grades of certificates, the county superintendent may grant permission to teach until the next regular examination, to any person applying at any other time than at a regular examination who can show satisfactory reasons for failing to attend such examination, subject to such rules and regulations as may be prescribed by the Superintendent of Public Instruction. Such permit shall not be granted more than once to any person. The written answers of all candidates for county certificates, after being duly examined by the county superintendent, shall be kept by him for the space of six months after such examination, and any candidate, thinking an injustice has been done him, may by paying a fee of two dollars into the institute fund of the county and notifying both the county superintendent and the Superintendent of Public Instruction of the same, have his papers re-examined by the Superintendent of Public Instruction; the county superintendent shall on receipt of such notice from such complaining candidate transfer such papers to the Superintendent of Public Instruction, who shall examine such answers, and, if such answers warrant it, shall instruct the county superintendent to issue to such candidate a county certificate of the proper grade, and the county superintendent shall carry out such instructions.

§ 121. (742.) QUALIFICATIONS OF TEACHERS. CONTRACTS, WHEN VOID.] No certificate or permit to teach shall be issued to any person under eighteen years of age and no first grade certificate shall be issued to any person under twenty years of age and who has not taught successfully twelve school months; and a third grade certificate shall not be issued more than twice to the same person. The certificate so issued by a county superintendent shall be valid only in the county where issued; *provided*, that a first grade certificate may be renewed once without examination at the discretion of the county superintendent, upon payment of the proper fee for the institute fund as provided in the case of examination; *provided, further*, that a first grade certificate shall be valid in any county of the State when indorsed by the county superintendent of such county. No person shall be employed or permitted to teach in any of the public schools of the State, except those in cities organized for school purposes under special laws, who is not the holder of a lawful certificate of qualification, or permit to teach; *provided, further*, that no certificate or permit to teach in the schools of the State shall be granted to any person not a citizen of the United States unless such person has resided in the United States for one year last prior to the time of such application for certificate or permit. Any contract made in violation of this section shall be void.

§ 122. (743.) FEE FOR CERTIFICATE.] Each applicant for a county certificate shall pay one dollar to the county superintendent, which shall be used by him in support of teachers' institutes in the county.

§ 123. (744.) CERTIFICATES, WHEN REVOCABLE.] The county superintendent is authorized and required to revoke and annul at any time a certificate granted by him or his predecessor for any cause which would have authorized or required him to refuse to grant it if known at the time it was granted, and for incompetency, immorality, intemperance, cruelty, crime against the law of the State, refusal to perform his duty, or general neglect of the business of the school. The revocation of the certificate shall terminate the employment of such teacher in the school where he may be at the time employed, but such teacher must be paid up to the time of receiving notice of such revocation. The superintendent must immediately notify the clerk of the school district where such teacher is employed and he may notify the teacher through the clerk of such revocation, and must enter his action in such case in the books of record in his office.

§ 124. (745.) PROCEEDINGS TO REVOKE. TEACHERS ALLOWED DEFENSE.] In proceedings to revoke a certificate the county superintendent may act upon his personal knowledge or upon competent evidence obtained from others. In the latter case, action shall be taken only after a fair hearing, and the teacher must be notified of the charge and given an opportunity to make a defense at such time and place as may be stated in such notice. Upon his own knowledge the superintendent may act immediately without notice, after an opportunity has been afforded such teacher for personal explanation. When any certificate is revoked the teacher shall return it to the superintendent, but if such teacher refuses or neglects so to do the superintendent may issue notice of such revocation by publication in some newspaper printed in the county.

## ARTICLE XII.

### DUTIES OF TEACHERS.

Section.
125. Give Notice of Opening and Closing School.
126. When Teacher Not Entitled to Compensation.
127. Teacher's Register, What to Contain.
128. School Year and School Week Defined.—Holidays.
129. Branches to be Taught in all Schools.

Section.
130. Teachers' Institutes, How Noticed—Penalty for Failure to Attend.
131. Pupil May be Suspended for Cause.
132. Assignment of Studies to Pupils.
133. Bible Not Sectarian Book, Reading Optional with Pupil.

§ 125. (746.) GIVE NOTICE OF OPENING AND CLOSING SCHOOL.] Each teacher on commencing a term of school shall give written notice to the county superintendent of the time and place of beginning such school and the time when it will probably close. If such school is to be suspended for one week or more in such term, the teacher shall notify the county superintendent of such suspension.

§ 126. (747.) WHEN TEACHER NOT ENTITLED TO COMPENSATION.] No teacher shall be entitled to or receive any compensation for the time he teaches in any public school without a certificate valid and in force for such time in the county where such school is taught, except that if a teacher's certificate shall expire by its own limitation within six weeks of the close of the term, such teacher may finish such term without re-examination or renewal of such certificate.

§ 127. (748.) TEACHER'S REGISTER, WHAT TO CONTAIN.] Each teacher shall keep a school register and at the close of each term make a report, containing the number of visits of the county superintendent, and such items and in such form as shall be required. Such report shall be made in duplicate, one copy of which shall be filed with the district clerk, and one copy sent to the county superintendent. No teacher shall be paid the last month's wages in any term until such report shall be filed with and be approved by the district clerk.

§ 128. (749.) SCHOOL YEAR AND SCHOOL WEEK DEFINED. HOLIDAYS.] The school year shall begin on the first day of January and close on the thirty-first day of December of each year. A school week shall consist of five days, and a school month of twenty days. No school shall be taught on a legal holiday nor on any Saturday. A legal holiday in term time falling upon a day which otherwise would be a school day shall be counted and the teacher shall be paid therefor, but no teacher shall be paid for Saturday, nor be permitted to teach on Saturday to make up for the loss of a day in the term.

§ 129. (750.) BRANCHES TO BE TAUGHT IN ALL SCHOOLS.] Each teacher in the common schools shall teach pupils, when they are sufficiently advanced to pursue the same, the following branches: Orthography, reading, spelling, writing, arithmetic, language lessons, English grammar, geography, United States history, civil government, physiology and hygiene, giving special instruction concerning the nature of alcoholic drinks, stimulants and narcotics, and their effect upon the human system; physiology and hygiene and the nature of alcoholic drinks, stimulants and narcotics and their effect upon the human system shall be taught as thoroughly as any branch is taught, by the use of a text book to all pupils able to use a text book who have not thoroughly studied that branch and orally to all other pupils. When such oral instruction is given as herein required, a sufficient time, not less than fifteen minutes, shall be given to such oral instruction for at least four days in each school week. Each teacher in special school districts and in cities organized for school purposes under special law shall conform to and be governed by the provisions of this section.

§ 130. (751.) TEACHERS' INSTITUTES, HOW NOTICED. PENALTY FOR FAILURE TO ATTEND.] When a teachers' institute is appointed to be held in any county, it shall be the duty of the county superintendent to give written or printed notice thereof to each teacher in the public schools of the county, and as far as possible to all others not then engaged in teaching who are holders of teachers' certificates at least ten days before the opening of such institute of the time and place of holding it. Each teacher receiving such notice engaged in teaching a term of school, which includes the time of holding such institute, shall close school during such institute and attend the same and shall be paid by the school board of the district his regular wages as teacher for the time (not less than four days) he attended such institute, as certified by the county superintendent or conductor of the institute. No teacher failing to attend such institute shall receive any compensation for the time he may have taught during the session of the same. The county superintendent may revoke the certificate of any teacher in his county for inexcusable neglect or refusal after due notice to attend a teacher's institute held for such county. The provisions of this section shall not apply to teachers in cities organized for school purposes under a special law.

§ 131. (752.) PUPIL MAY BE SUSPENDED FOR CAUSE.] A teacher may suspend from school for not more than five days any pupil for insubordination or habitual disobedience, or disorderly conduct. In such case the teacher shall give immediate notice to the parent or guardian of such pupil, also to some member of the district school board of such suspension and the reason therefor.

§ 132. (753.) ASSIGNMENT OF STUDIES TO PUPILS.] It shall

be the duty of the teacher to assign to each pupil such studies as he is qualified to pursue, and to place him in the proper class in any studies subject to the provisions in section 750; *provided*, that in a graded school under the charge of a principal or local superintendent, such principal or superintendent shall perform this duty. In case any parent or guardian is dissatisfied with such assignment or classification, the matter shall be referred to and decided by the county superintendent.

§ 133. (754.) BIBLE NOT SECTARIAN BOOK, READING OPTIONAL WITH PUPIL.] The Bible shall not be deemed a sectarian book. It shall not be excluded from any public school. It may at the option of the teacher be read in school without sectarian comment, not to exceed ten minutes daily. No pupil shall be required to read it nor be present in the school room during the reading thereof contrary to the wishes of his parents or guardian or other person having him in charge. Moral instruction tending to impress upon the minds of pupils the importance of truthfulness, temperance, purity, public spirit, patriotism, and respect for honest labor, obedience to parents and due deference for old age, shall be given by each teacher in the public schools.

## ARTICLE XIII.

### INSTITUTES, ASSOCIATIONS AND READING CIRCLE.

Section.
134. Teachers' Institutes—Apportionment of Funds.
135. Appropriation for Institute Fund—Designation of Conductors.

Section.
136. Institute Funds, How Paid Out.
137. County Commissioners May Aid Institutes.

§ 134. (755.) TEACHERS' INSTITUTES. APPORTIONMENT OF FUNDS.] All money received by the county superintendent from examination fees shall constitute an institute fund for the county and shall be used by him to aid in the support of teachers' institutes to be held within and for the county, and to pay necessary expenses incurred therein. The county superintendent shall, at the end of each year, submit a full and accurate statement of the receipts and expenditures of these funds, verified by his oath, to the Superintendent of Public Instruction; *provided*, that the several persons designated as herein provided, to act as conductors of teachers' institutes shall, at the close of each series of institutes, certify to the Superintendent of Public Instruction an itemized statement of all actual and necessary expenses incurred by such conductor in the discharge of his duties as such, and such superintendent shall apportion such total expense among the several counties in which such conductor was assigned to conduct the institute, in proportion to the average attendance at such institute, but by such apportionment no county shall be proportioned a greater amount than the amount of the county institute fund on hand. The county superintendent shall present a bill to the county auditor for the amount of such expense apportioned to his county, and the auditor shall issue a warrant therefor as provided by law. All additional compensation and other incidental expenses of such county institute, except as provided by the State appropriation, shall be paid out of the county institute fund.

§ 135. (756.) APPROPRIATION FOR INSTITUTE FUND. DESIGNATION OF CONDUCTORS.] There is hereby appropriated out of any funds in the State Treasury, not otherwise appropriated, the sum of fifty dollars each year to each organized county in the State in which there are ten or more resident teachers, which shall be designated as the State Institute Fund and which shall be used exclusively in employing persons of learning, ability and experience as conductors of teachers' institutes, and the further · sum of ten cents a mile for the distance actually and necessarily traveled by a lecturer for such institute. The Superintendent of Public Instruction after consultation with the county superintendents as to the special needs and wants of their respective counties, shall appoint the time, place and duration of these institutes and shall designate the persons to act as conductors of and lecturers at such institutes, as in his judgment the needs of the various counties demand.

§ 136. (757.) INSTITUTE FUNDS, HOW PAID OUT.] It shall be the duty of the county superintendent in all cases to consult with the Superintendent of Public Instruction in reference to the management of such institute, and as far as practicable, to carry out the suggestions of such superintendent as to the modes of instruction. No salary shall be paid to any conductor of any institute not previously appointed or employed as herein provided. The money hereby appropriated from the State Treasury for the support of teachers' institutes shall be paid to the persons to whom it is due by warrant of the State Auditor upon the State Treasurer, which shall be issued upon the presentation of an account in due form receipted by the person to whom due and approved by the Superintendent of Public Instruction; *provided*, that no county shall receive more than ten dollars from such appropriation for the payment of conductor's salary for each day its institute is in session.

§ 137. (758.) COUNTY COMMISSIONERS MAY AID INSTITUTES.] The money assigned for any particular institute may be added to any fund furnished for the purpose by any county, and the institute extended as long as the entire fund will allow. If a sufficient county fund is not otherwise provided, the board of county commissioners may appropriate not more than fifty dollars in any county each year in aid of institutes. The Superintendent of Public Instruction may require a statement of the amount of funds the county has on hand for this purpose at any time.

# ARTICLE XIV.

## COMPULSORY ATTENDANCE.

Section.
138. School Age—Who Exempt from Compulsory Attendance.
139. Penalty.
140. Prosecution for Neglecting this Duty.

Section.
141. Child Labor Prohibited During School Hours.
142. Penalty for Violation.
143. Prosecutions, How Brought.

§ 138. (759.) SCHOOL AGE. WHO EXEMPT FROM COMPULSORY ATTENDANCE.] Every parent, guardian or other person having control of any child between eight and fourteen years of age, shall be required to send such child to a public school in the district, city or village in which he resides at least twelve weeks in each school year, six weeks of which shall be consecutive; and every parent, guardian or other person having control of any deaf child or youth between seven and twenty-one years of age, shall be required to send such child to the school for the deaf at the city of Devils Lake, for at least eight months in each school year; *provided*, that such parent, guardian or other person having control of any child shall be excused from such duty by the school board of the district or the board of education of the city or village, whenever it shall be shown to their satisfaction, subject to appeal as provided by law, that one of the following reasons therefor exists:

1. That such child is taught for the same length of time in a private school, approved by such board; but no school shall be approved by such board unless the branches usually taught in the public schools are taught in such school.

2. That such child has already acquired the branches of learning taught in the public schools.

3. That such child is in such a physical or mental condition (as declared by the county physician if required by the board,) as to render such attendance inexpedient or impracticable. If no school is taught the requisite length of time within two and one-half miles of the residence of such child by the nearest route, such attendance will not be enforced but this provision shall not apply to deaf children in the State. The common schools provided for in this chapter shall be at all times equally free, open and accessible to all children over six and under twenty years of age, residents of the school districts where they are held, or entitled to attend school under any special provisions of this chapter, subject to the regulations herein made and to such regulations as the several school boards and boards of education may prescribe equitably and justly and not in conflict with the provisions of law.

§ 139. (760.) PENALTY.] Any such parent, guardian or other person failing to comply with the requirements of the foregoing section, shall upon conviction thereof be deemed guilty of a misdemeanor, and shall be fined in a sum not less than five nor more than twenty dollars for the first offense and not less than ten dollars nor more than fifty dollars for the second and every subsequent offense with costs in each case.

§ 140. (761.) PROSECUTION FOR NEGLECTING THIS DUTY.] It shall be the duty of the president of the board of education of any city, town or village, or the president of the school board of any district, to inquire into all cases of neglect of the duty prescribed in this article and ascertain from the person neglecting to perform such duty, the reason therefor, if any, and shall forthwith proceed to secure the prosecution of any offense occurring under this article, and any such president neglecting to secure such prosecution for such offense within fifteen days after a written notice has been served by any taxpayer in such city, town, village or district, unless such person so complained of shall be excused by the board of education or school board for one of the reasons hereinbefore stated, he shall be deemed guilty of misdemeanor, and upon conviction shall be fined in a sum not less than five nor more than twenty dollars.

§ 141. (762.) CHILD LABOR PROHIBITED DURING SCHOOL HOURS.] No child between eight and fourteen years of age shall be employed in any mine, factory or workshop or mercantile establishment, or, except by his parents or guardian, in any other manner, during the hours when the public schools in the city, village or district are in session, unless the person employing him shall first procure a certificate from the superintendent of schools of the city or village, if one is employed, otherwise from the clerk of the school board or board of education, stating that such child has attended school for the period of twelve weeks during the year, as required by law, or has been excused from attendance as provided in section 759; and it shall be the duty of such superintendent or clerk to furnish such certificate upon application of the parent, guardian or other persons having control of such child, entitled to the same.

§ 142. (763.) PENALTY FOR VIOLATION.] Each owner, superintendent or overseer of any mine, factory, workshop or mercantile establishment, and any other person who shall employ any child between eight and fourteen years of age contrary to the provisions of this article, is guilty of a misdemeanor, and upon conviction thereof shall be fined for each offense in a sum not less than twenty nor more than fifty dollars and costs. Each person authorized to sign a certificate as prescribed in the preceding section, who certifies to any materially false statement therein, shall be fined not less than twenty nor more than fifty dollars and costs.

§ 143. (764.) PROSECUTIONS, HOW BROUGHT.] Prosecutions under this article shall be brought in the name of the State of North Dakota before any court of competent jurisdiction, and the fines collected shall be paid over to the county treasurer and by him credited to the general school fund of the State.

# ARTICLE XV.

## FINES, FORFEITURES AND PENALTIES.

Section.
144. Penalty for Neglect of Duty by School Director, Treasurer or Clerk.
145. Penalty for False Election Returns.
146. Speculation in Office Prohibited.
147. Penalty for Unlawful Drawing of School Money.
148. Use of School Funds—When Embezzlement.
149. Action to Recover Money when Treasurer Fails to Pay Over.

Section.
150. Penalty, when Indorsement of Unpaid Warrants is not Made.
151. Penalty for False Reports.
152. Penalty for Willful Disturbance of Public School.
153. Proposals for Contracts.

§ 144. (765.) PENALTY FOR NEGLECT OF DUTY BY SCHOOL DIRECTOR, TREASURER OR CLERK.] Each person duly elected to the office of director, treasurer or clerk of any district, who, having entered upon the duties of his office, shall neglect or refuse to perform any duties required of him by the provisions of this chapter shall upon conviction be fined in the sum of ten dollars, and his office shall be deemed vacant.

§ 145. (766.) PENALTY FOR FALSE ELECTION RETURNS.] Any judge or clerk of election, school district clerk or county auditor who willfully violates the provisions of this chapter in relation to elections or who willfully makes a false return shall upon conviction be deemed guilty of a felony.

§ 146. (767.) SPECULATION IN OFFICE PROHIBITED.] No school officer shall personally engage in the purchase of any school bonds or warrants, nor shall any such officer be personally interested in any contract requiring the expenditure of school funds, except for the purchase of fuel and such supplies as are in daily use, but not including furniture, or the expenditure of funds appropriated by the State, county, school corporation or otherwise for any school purpose connected with his office. Any violation of this section shall be a misdemeanor.

§ 147. (768.) PENALTY FOR UNLAWFUL DRAWING OF SCHOOL MONEY.] Any person who draws money from the county treasury, who is not at the time a duly qualified treasurer of the school corporation for which he draws the money and authorized to act as such, shall be guilty of a misdemeanor and shall upon conviction thereof be punished by a fine of not less than twenty-five dollars.

§ 148. (769.) USE OF SCHOOL FUNDS. WHEN EMBEZZLEMENT.] Each treasurer who shall loan any portion of the money in his hands belonging to any school district, whether for consideration or not, or who shall expend any portion thereof for his own or any other person's private use, is guilty of embezzlement, and no such treasurer shall pay over or deliver the school money in his hands to any officer or person or to any committee to be expended by him or them; but all public funds shall be paid out only by the proper treasurer as hereinbefore provided.

§ 149. (770.) ACTION TO RECOVER MONEY WHEN TREASURER FAILS TO PAY OVER.] If any person shall refuse or neglect to pay over any money in his hands as treasurer of a school district to his successor in office his successor must, without delay, bring action upon the official bond of such treasurer for the recovery of such money.

§ 150. (771.) PENALTY, WHEN INDORSEMENT OF UNPAID WARRANTS IS NOT MADE.] Any violation by a district treasurer of the provisions of this chapter requiring indorsement of warrants not paid for want of funds, and the payment thereof in the order of presentation and indorsement, is a misdemeanor, punishable by a fine not exceeding one hundred dollars.

§ 151. (772.) PENALTY FOR FALSE REPORTS.] Each clerk or treasurer of a district who willfully signs or transmits a false report to the county superintendent or willfully signs, issues or publishes a false statement of facts purporting or appearing to be based upon the books, accounts or records or of the affairs, resources and credit of the district shall upon conviction be punished by a fine not exceeding fifty dollars or by imprisonment in the county jail not exceeding fifteen days.

§ 152. (773.) PENALTY FOR WILLFUL DISTURBANCE OF PUBLIC SCHOOL.] Each person, whether pupil or not, who willfully molests or disturbs a public school when in session or who willfully interferes with or interrupts the proper order or management of a public school by act of violence, boisterous conduct or threatening language, so as to prevent the teacher or any pupil from performing his duty, or who shall in the presence of the school or school children upbraid, insult or threaten the teacher shall upon conviction thereof be punished by a fine not exceeding twenty-five dollars or by imprisonment in the county jail for a period not exceeding ten days, or by both.

§ 153. (774.) PROPOSALS FOR CONTRACTS.] No contract, except for teachers' or janitors' wages, involving the expenditure of school funds or money appropriated for any purpose relating to the educational system of this State or any county, district or school corporation therein, when the amount exceeds one hundred dollars, shall be let until proposals are advertised for, and after such advertisement, only to the lowest responsible bidder. Any violation of this section shall be a misdemeanor.

## ARTICLE XVI.

### BONDS.

Section.
154. Schools Bonds, How Issued.
155. Notice of Election to Vote Bonds.
156. Bonds, Denomination of—Interest—Limit of Issue.
157. Bonds, Record of to be Kept.
158. Sinking Fund and Interest Tax.

Section.
159. Bonds, How Negotiated.
160. County Auditor may Levy Tax to Pay Bonds, When.
161. Canceled Bonds, Record of.
162. Proposals for Building School Houses.
163. Provisions of this Article, How Applicable.

§ 154. (775.) SCHOOL BONDS, HOW ISSUED.] Whenever a duly constituted school district in any organized county in the

State at any regular or special meeting held for that purpose shall determine, by a majority vote of all the qualified voters of such school district present at such meeting and voting, to issue school district bonds for the purpose of building and furnishing a school house and purchasing grounds on which to locate the same, or to fund any outstanding indebtedness, the district school board may lawfully issue such bonds in accordance with the provisions of this article.

§ 155. (776.) NOTICE OF ELECTION TO VOTE BONDS.] Before the question of issuing bonds shall be submitted to a vote of the school district, notices shall be posted in at least three public and conspicuous places in such district stating the time and place of such meeting, the amount of bonds proposed to be issued, and the time in which they shall be made payable Such notices shall be posted at least twenty days before the meeting, and the voting shall be done by means of written or printed ballots, and all ballots deposited in favor of issuing bonds shall have thereon the words "for issuing bonds," and those opposed thereto shall have thereon the words "against issuing bonds" and if a majority of all the votes cast shall be in favor of issuing bonds the school board, through its proper officers shall forthwith issue bonds in accordance with such vote; but if a majority of all votes cast are against issuing bonds then no further action can be had and the question shall not be again submitted to a vote for one year thereafter except for a different amount; *provided*, that the question of issuing bonds shall not be submitted to a vote of the district and no meeting shall be called for that purpose until the district school board shall have been petitioned in writing by at least one-third of the voters of the district.

§ 156. (777.) BONDS, DENOMINATION OF. INTEREST. LIMIT OF ISSUE.] The denomination of the bonds which may be issued under the provisions of this article shall be fifty dollars or some multiple of fifty not exceeding five hundred dollars and shall bear interest at the rate of not exceeding seven per cent per annum, payable semi-annually in accordance with interest coupons which shall be attached to such bonds; and no greater amount than one thousand dollars can be issued for any one school house, except in towns and villages of more than three hundred inhabitants, and in such districts the amount shall not exceed four per cent of its assessed valuation, and may be made payable in not less than ten nor more than twenty years from their date.

§ 157. (778.) BONDS, RECORD OF TO BE KEPT.] Whenever any bonds are issued under the provisions of this chapter they shall be lithographed or printed on bond paper and shall state upon their face the date of their issue, the amount of the bonds, to whom and for what purpose issued, also the time and place of payment and the rate of interest to be paid. They shall have printed upon the margin the words "Authorized by article 16 of chapter 9 of the political code of North Dakota of 1895."

Immediately after the issuing of school bonds pursuant to this chapter the clerk of the school district so issuing its bonds shall file with the county auditor of the county in which such district is situated, certified copies of all the proceedings had in such district relative to the issuing of such bonds and also a statement of the amount of the indebtedness of such school district; and before any of the bonds are disposed of they shall be presented to the county auditor of the county in which the school district issuing the same is situated. He shall carefully examine the records of the proceedings of such school district upon the question of issuing such bonds as the same are filed with him as hereinbefore directed, and shall satisfy himself by the evidence thus furnished whether or not all the laws of the state relative to the issuing of such bonds have been complied with. If satisfied that they have been and that the bonds in question have been legally issued, he shall in a book kept for such purpose preserve a register of each bond showing in separate columns the name of the school district issuing the bonds, the number of such bonds, the denomination thereof, the date of their issue, the date when they will mature, the names of the school officers executing the same and such other facts as may be pertinent, and he shall then indorse on each of such bonds the following certificate:

State of North Dakota, } ss.
County of ........... }

I,..............., county auditor, do hereby certify that the within bond is issued pursuant to law and is within the debt limit prescribed by the Constitution of the State of North Dakota and in accordance with the vote of ........school district,........ at a ........ (regular or special) meeting held on the ........ day of ........ A. D. 189..., to issue bonds to the amount of ............dollars, and is a legal and valid debt of such school district; that such bonds are duly registered in this office and that such school district is legally organized and the signatures affixed to such bonds are the genuine signatures of the proper officers of such school district.

The blanks shall be filled according to the facts and the certificate officially signed by the county auditor and attested by his official seal. Such bonds shall be signed by the president and clerk of the school board and shall be registered in a book to be kept by the clerk for that purpose in which shall be entered the number, date and name of the person to whom issued and the date when the same will become due.

§ 158. (779.) SINKING FUND AND INTEREST TAX.] In addition to the amount that may already be assessed under existing laws, there shall be levied upon the taxable property of the school districts so issuing bonds at or before their issuance and collected as other taxes are collected, a sum sufficient, not exceeding five mills on the dollar of assessed valuation of such districts, to pay interest upon such bonded indebtedness, and after five years in like manner a further tax not exceeding two mills on the dollar for a sinking fund to be used in payment of such bonds when they become due and for no other purpose, except that whenever there are sufficient funds on hand belonging to such sinking fund the school board may, in its discretion, purchase any of its outstanding bonds at their market value and pay for the same out of such sinking fund.

§ 159. (780.) BONDS, HOW NEGOTIATED.] When any bonds shall be issued under the provisions of this article, the school district treasurer shall have authority to negotiate and sell such bonds for not less than par, and the proceeds shall be used exclusively for the purpose of building and furnishing a school house and in payment for a site for the same, and for the necessary outbuildings.

§ 160. (781.) COUNTY AUDITOR MAY LEVY TAX TO PAY BONDS, WHEN.] When any school board neglects or refuses to levy a tax in accordance with law to meet outstanding bonds or the interest thereon, the county auditor shall have power to levy such tax and when collected to apply the proceeds to the payment of such coupons and bonds.

§ 161. (782.) CANCELED BONDS, RECORD OF.] When the bonds of any school district shall have been paid by the school board they shall be canceled by writing or printing in red ink the words "canceled and paid" across each bond and coupon and the date of payment and the amount paid shall be entered in the clerk's register against the proper number of the bonds, and the bonds so canceled shall be filed in the office of the district treasurer until all the outstanding bonds are paid, when they shall be destroyed in the presence of the full board.

§ 162. (783.) PROPOSALS FOR BUILDING SCHOOL HOUSES.] When any school house is built with funds provided for in the manner herein authorized, the school board shall advertise at least thirty days in some newspaper printed in the county, or by posting notices for the same length of time in at least three of the most public and conspicuous places if no newspaper is published in the county, for sealed proposals for building and furnishing such school house in accordance with plans and specifications furnished by the school board, reserving the right to reject any and all bids, and if any of the proposals shall be reasonable and satisfactory such board shall award the contract to the lowest responsible bidder and shall require of such contractor a bond in double the amount of the contract, conditioned that he will properly account for all money and property of the school district that may come into his hands and that he will perform the conditions of his contract in a faithful manner and in accordance with its provisions; and in case all the proposals are rejected, such board shall advertise anew in the same manner as before until a reasonable bid shall be submitted.

§ 163. (784.) Provisions of this article, how applicable.] The provisions of this article shall be applicable to and authorize the issuance of bonds by such school districts as have already built school houses and issued orders or warrants therefor and any such school district may vote to bond the indebtedness incurred by reason of building and furnishing a school house and purchasing a site for the same and bonds may be issued in the same manner as hereinbefore provided for building and furnishing school houses.

## ARTICLE XVII.

### SPECIAL DISTRICTS.

Section.
164. Cities Governed by the Provisions of this Article.
165. Adjacent Territory, How Attached for School Purposes.
166. Name of Body Corporate.
167. Conveyance of School Property, How Executed.
168. Special School Districts, How Organized.
169. Election of Board of Education.
170. Terms of Office—Quorum.
171. Members not to be Interested in School Contracts.
172. Annual and Special Meetings of Board.
173. Organization of Board.
174. Duties of President.
175. Duties of Clerk—Records.
176. Powers and Duties of Board.
177. Treasurer, Custodian of School Moneys.
178. Schools Under Supervision of Whom.
179. Taxable Property.
180. Annual School Tax.
181. Expenditures—Contracts.
182. Treasurer.
183. Treasurer, Duties of.
184. Treasurer's Bond.

Section.
185. Board Assumes Control After Equalization of Debts and Property.
186. Special District may Become Part of General District, When.
187. Election of Boards of Education in Special Districts.
188. Notice of Election, Contents of.
189. Notice of Election, Form of.
190. Election Precincts and Officers of Election.
191. Canvass of Returns.
192. Certificates of Election.
193. Vacancies, How Filled.
194. Oath of Office.
195. Bonds, How and When may be Issued.
196. Election for Issuing Bonds.
197. Bonds to Specify What—Debt Limit.
198. Levy for Interest and Sinking Fund.
199. Investment of Sinking Fund.
200. Interest Coupons.
201. Security for Payment of Bonds.
202. Bond Register.
203. Refunding Bonds, Issuance of.
204. Bonds may be Exchanged.
205. Issue of Bonds, How Governed.
206. Surplus Funds, How Transferred.

§ 164. (785.) Cities governed by the provisions of this article.] All cities and incorporated towns and villages which have heretofore been organized under the general school laws and which are provided with a board of education shall be governed by the provisions of this article. Any city or incorporated town or village having a population of over three hundred inhabitants may be constituted a special school district in the manner hereinafter prescribed, and shall then be governed by the provisions of this article; *provided*, that any city heretofore organized for school purposes under a special act may adopt the provisions of this article by a majority vote of the voters therein, in the same manner as is provided for the organization of a new corporation under the provisions of this article.

§ 165. (786.) Adjacent territory, how attached for school purposes.] When any city, town or village has been organized for school purposes and provided with a board of education under any general school law, or a special act, or under the provisions of this article, territory outside the limits thereof but adjacent thereto may be attached to such city, town or village for school purposes by the board of education thereof upon application in writing signed by a majority of the voters of such adjacent territory; and upon such application being made, if such board shall deem it proper and to the best interests of the schools of such corporation and of the territory to be attached, an order shall be issued by such board attaching such adjacent territory to such corporation for school purposes, and the same shall be entered upon the records of the board. Such territory shall from the date of such order be and compose a part of such corporation for school purposes only; such adjacent territory shall be attached for voting purposes to such corporation, or if the school election is held in wards, to the ward or wards or election precinct or precincts to which it lies adjacent; and the voters thereof shall vote only for school offices and upon school questions.

§ 166. (787.) NAME OF BODY CORPORATE.] Every such district shall be a body corporate for school purposes by the name of "The board of education of the city, town or village (as the case may be) of ........(here insert the corporate name of the city, town or village) of the State of North Dakota," and shall possess all the powers and duties usual to corporations for public purposes or conferred upon it by this article or which may hereafter be conferred upon it by law; and in such name it may sue and be sued, contract and be contracted with, and hold and convey such real and personal property as shall come into its possession by will or otherwise; and it shall procure and keep a corporate seal by which its official acts may be attested.

§ 167. (788.) CONVEYANCE OF SCHOOL PROPERTY, HOW EXECUTED.] Any such city or incorporated town or village is authorized and required, upon the request of the board of education, to convey to such board of education all property within the limits of any such corporation heretofore purchased by ·it for school purposes and now held and used for such purposes, the title to which is vested in any such civil corporation. All conveyances for such property shall be signed by the mayor or president of the board of trustees and attested by the clerk of such corporation, and shall have the seal of the corporation affixed thereto and be acknowledged by the mayor or president in the same manner as other conveyances of real estate.

§ 168. (789.) SPECIAL SCHOOL DISTRICTS, HOW ORGANIZED.] When a petition signed by one-third of the voters of a city or incorporated town or village entitled to vote at such election is presented to the council or board of trustees thereof asking that such city, town or village be organized as a special school district, such council or board of trustees shall order an election for such purpose, notice of which shall be given and the election conducted and the returns made in the manner provided by law for the annual election of municipal officers of such corporation;

and the voters thereof shall vote for or against organization as a special school district at such election.

§ 169. (790.) ELECTION OF BOARD OF EDUCATION.] If a majority of the votes cast at such election is for organization as a special school district another election shall be called in the same manner as is prescribed in the foregoing section, at which the voters of such city, town or village shall elect five members of the board of education, two of whom shall serve until the first annual election, two until the second annual election and one until the third annual election thereafter and until their successors are elected and qualified; and their respective terms shall be determined by lot.

§ 170. (791.) TERMS OF OFFICE. QUORUM. The board of education of each special district shall consist of five members who shall be elected by the legal voters thereof and who shall hold their office for the term of three years and until their successors are elected and qualified, except as provided for first elections under this article, and three members shall constitute a quorum for the transaction of business at any legal meeting.

§ 171. (792.) MEMBERS NOT TO BE INTERESTED IN SCHOOL CONTRACTS.] The members of such board shall receive no compensation, and shall not be interested, directly or indirectly, in any contract for making any improvements or repairs or for erecting any building or for furnishing any material or supplies for their district.

§ 172. (793.) ANNUAL AND SPECIAL MEETINGS OF BOARD.] The annual meeting of such board of education shall be held on the second Tuesday in July following the annual election, at which time the newly elected members shall assume the duties of their office. Each board shall meet for the transaction of business as often as once in each calendar month thereafter and may adjourn for a shorter time. Special meetings may be called by the president or in his absence by any two members of the board by giving a personal notice to each member of the board or by causing a written or printed notice to be left at his last place of residence at least forty-eight hours before the time of such meeting.

§ 173. (794.) ORGANIZATION OF BOARD.] At the annual meeting on the second Tuesday in July of each year such board of education shall organize by electing a president from among its members who shall serve for one year; and they shall also elect a clerk, not one of their own number, who shall hold his office during the pleasure of the board and receive such compensation for his services as shall be fixed by the board. In the absence of the president at any meeting, a president *pro tempore* may be elected by the board.

§ 174. (795.) DUTIES OF PRESIDENT.] The president shall preside at all meetings of the board, appoint all committees · whose appointment is not otherwise provided for and sign all warrants ordered by the board to be drawn upon the treasurer for school moneys and perform other acts required by law.

§ 175. (796.) DUTIES OF CLERK. RECORDS.] The clerk shall keep a true record of all the proceedings of the board, take charge of its books and documents, countersign all warrants for school moneys drawn upon the treasurer by order of the board and affix the corporate seal thereto and perform such other duties as the board may require. The records, books, vouchers and papers of the board shall be open to examination by any taxpayer of the district. Such record or a transcript thereof certified by the clerk and attested by the seal of the board, shall be received in all courts as *prima facie* evidence of the facts therein set forth.

§ 176. (797.) POWERS AND DUTIES OF BOARD.] Each board of education shall have power and it shall be its duty:

1. To establish a system of graded common schools, which shall be free to all children of legal school age residing within such special district, and shall be kept open not less than six nor more than ten months in any year.

2. To establish and maintain such schools in its city, town or village as it shall deem requisite or expedient and to change or discontinue the same.

3. To establish and maintain a high school, whenever in its opinion the educational interests of the corporation demand the same, in which such courses of study shall be pursued as shall be prescribed or approved by the Superintendent of Public Instruction, together with such additional courses as such board of education may thereafter deem advisable to establish.

4. To purchase, sell, exchange and hire school houses and rooms, lots or sites for school houses, and to fence and otherwise improve them as it deems proper.

5. Upon such lots and upon such sites as may be owned by such special district to build, alter, enlarge, improve and repair school houses, outhouses and appurtenances as it may deem advisable.

6. To purchase, sell, exchange, improve and repair school apparatus, text-books for the use of the pupils, furniture and appendages, and to provide fuel for the schools.

· 7. To have the custody of all school property of every kind and to see that the ordinances and by-laws of the city or village in relation thereto are observed.

8. To contract with, employ and pay all teachers in such schools and to dismiss and remove for cause any teacher whenever the interests of the school may require it; but any such teacher shall be required to hold a certificate to teach, issued by the county superintendent or the Superintendent of Public Instruction, and if any such teacher holds only a county certificate the board may impose such further requirements as the best interests

S. L.—6.

of the several grades may require. No person who is a relative of any member of the board shall be employed as teacher without the concurrence of the entire board.

9. To employ, should it deem it expedient, a competent and discreet person as superintendent of schools and to fix and pay a proper compensation therefor, and such superintendent may be required to act as principal or teacher in such schools.

10. To defray the necessary and contingent expenses of the board, including the compensation of its clerk.

11. To adopt, alter and repeal, whenever it may deem expedient, rules and regulations for organization, grading, government and instruction and the reception of pupils, their suspension and expulsion and their transfer from one school to another. But no pupil shall be suspended or expelled except for insubordination, habitual disobedience or disorderly conduct; such suspension shall not be for a longer period than ten days, nor such expulsion beyond the end of the current term of school.

12. Each member shall visit, at least twice in each year, all the public schools in the city or village.

13. To make a report on January first, or as soon thereafter as practicable, of the progress, prosperity and condition, financial as well as educational, of all the schools under its charge, a copy of which, together with such further information as shall be required by the Superintendent of Public Instruction, shall be forwarded to the county superintendent the same as reports are made by other school districts; and such report or such portion thereof as the board of education shall consider advantageous to the public, shall be published in a newspaper in the city or village, and in cities and villages of over eight hundred inhabitants, it may be published in pamphlet form.

14. To admit children of persons not living in such special district into the schools of such district, and to fix and collect the tuition therefor, if in its judgment the best interests of the school will permit.

15. To cause an enumeration of the children of school age within such special district, including those residing in any territory thereto attached for school purposes, to be made annually, as provided for other school districts, and return the same to the county superintendent.

§ 177. (798.) TREASURER, CUSTODIAN OF SCHOOL MONEYS.] All moneys from whatever source, which the board of education of any special district shall by law be authorized to receive, shall be paid over to the treasurer of such board and he shall charge the same to the proper fund.

§ 178. (799.) SCHOOLS UNDER SUPERVISION OF WHOM.] The schools of each special district shall be under the immediate supervision of the board of education or the school superintendent appointed by such board, subject to such general directions and supervision by the county superintendent as are provided for in this chapter.

§ 179. (800.) TAXABLE PROPERTY.] The taxable property of the whole school corporation including the territory attached for school purposes, shall be subject to taxation. All taxes collected for the benefit of the school shall be paid in money, and shall be placed in the hands of the treasurer, subject to the order of the board of education.

§ 180. (801.) ANNUAL SCHOOL TAX.] The board of education shall on or before the twentieth day of July of each year levy a tax for the support of the schools of the corporation, including any expenditures allowed by law, for the fiscal year next ensuing, not exceeding in any one year thirty mills on the dollar on all the real and personal property within the district which is taxable according to the laws of this State, the amount of which levy the clerk of the board shall certify to the county auditor, who is authorized and required to place the same on the tax roll of such county to be collected by the county treasurer as other taxes and paid over by him to the treasurer of the board of education, of whom he shall take a receipt in duplicate, one of which he shall file in his office and the other he shall forthwith transmit to the clerk of the board of education.

§ 181. (802.) EXPENDITURES. CONTRACTS.] No expenditures involving an amount greater than one hundred dollars shall be made except in accordance with the provisions of a written contract, and no contract involving an expenditure of more than five hundred dollars for the purpose of erecting any public buildings or making any improvements shall be made except upon sealed proposals and to the lowest responsible bidder, after public notice for ten days previous to receiving such bids.

§ 182. (803.) TREASURER.] The treasurer of any city, town or village comprising a special district shall be treasurer of the board of education thereof.

§ 183. (804.) TREASURER, DUTIES OF.] The treasurer of each board of education shall keep a true account of the receipts and expenditures of the various funds separately, and shall prepare and submit in writing a quarterly report of the state of the finances of the district; and shall, when required, produce at any meeting of such board or any committee appointed for the purpose of examining his accounts, all books and papers pertaining to his office. He shall safely keep in his possession or under his control all school moneys coming into his hands, and shall pay out such moneys only upon a warrant signed by the president, countersigned by the clerk and attested by the corporate seal of the board.

§ 184. (805.) TREASURER'S BOND.] The treasurer of the board shall execute a bond to such board, with sufficient sureties to be approved by the board, in such sum and as such board may from time to time require, as near as can be ascertained in double the amount of the moneys likely to come into his hands, conditioned for the faithful discharge of his duties as treasurer; which bond shall be in addition to his bond to the city, town or village. In case of the failure of the city, town or village treasurer to give such bond within ten days after being required so to do by such board of education, such treasurer's office shall become vacant, and the council or board of trustees of such city, town or village shall appoint another person in his place, who shall give such additional bond.

§ 185. (806.) BOARD ASSUMES CONTROL AFTER EQUALIZATION OF DEBTS AND PROPERTY.] When any board of education shall be organized under the provisions of this article, it shall, after the equalization hereinafter provided for, assume control of the schools of the city, town or village and shall be entitled to the possession of all property of the former district or districts or parts thereof lying within such city, town or village, for the use of schools. Such board shall also be entitled to its due proportion of all moneys on hand and taxes already levied but not collected, and shall be liable for a proper amount of the debts and liabilities of such former district, to be determined in the manner provided in this chapter for the equalization, determination and division of debts, property and assets of school districts consolidated or divided.

§ 186. (807.) SPECIAL DISTRICT MAY BECOME PART OF GENERAL DISTRICT, WHEN.] Any special district organized under the general school laws and provided with a board of education may become a part of the school district in which it is located, whenever it is so decided by a majority vote of the school electors of the city, town or village and of such school district voting at an election called for that purpose. An election for such purpose shall be ordered and proper notice thereof given by the board of education and the school board of such district in the same manner as is required for the election of school officers in such district, when petitioned by one-third of the voters resident in such district, and when so united the determination and division of the debts, property and assets shall be made by arbitration as provided in this chapter for school districts consolidated or divided. Villages not incorporated but heretofore organized under the general school laws and provided with a board of education shall become a part of the school district in which they are located and the determination and division of the property, debts and assets shall be made by arbitration as aforesaid.

§ 187. (808.) ELECTION OF BOARDS OF EDUCATION IN SPECIAL DISTRICTS.] On the third Tuesday in June each year an election shall be held in each special district at which such members of the board of education shall be elected at large as shall be necessary to fill all vacancies therein caused by expiration of terms of office or otherwise, and each member elected shall serve for a term of three years commencing on the second Tuesday in July following his election and until his successor is elected and qualified, except when elected to serve an unexpired term. The polls shall be open at 9 o'clock A. M. and kept open until 4 o'clock P. M. on the day of such election.

§ 188. (809.) NOTICE OF ELECTION, CONTENTS OF.] Such election shall be called by the board of education of such special district, which shall cause notice thereof to be posted or published as required by law for the annual election of civil officers in the city, town or village comprising such special district; such notice shall be signed by the clerk, or, in his absence, by the president of the board of education of such district, and shall state the time and place of holding such election and what officers are to be elected and their terms.

§ 189. (810.) NOTICE OF ELECTION, FORM OF.] Such notice shall be in substantially the following form:

Notice is hereby given, that on Tuesday the.......day of June A. D......, an annual election will be held at ........ (here insert polling place) for the purpose of electing the following members of the board of education.........(here insert terms for which they are to be elected), for the city, town or village of.......... (here insert name) and the polls will be open at nine o'clock A. M. and closed at four o'clock P. M. of that day.

By order of the board of education.

Signed......................
· Clerk.

§ 190. (811.) ELECTION PRECINCTS AND OFFICERS OF ELECTION.] At least fifteen days prior to such election the board of education of each special district shall designate one polling place and appoint two persons to act as judges and two persons to act as clerks. Before opening the polls each of such judges and clerks shall take an oath that he will perform his duties as judge or clerk (as the case may be) according to law and to the best of his ability, which oath may be administered by any officer authorized to administer oaths or by either of said judges or clerks to the others.

§ 191. (812.) CANVASS OF RETURNS.] Such election shall be conducted and the votes canvassed in the manner provided by law for elections of county officers, and returns shall be made showing the number of votes cast for each person for any office, which shall be signed by the judges and clerks of election, and the person receiving the highest number of votes for each office in the district shall be declared elected, and the returns shall be filed with the clerk of the board of education within two days thereafter.

§ 192. (813.) CERTIFICATES OF ELECTION.] The clerk of the board shall give to each person elected at such election a certificate stating that he was duly elected as a member of the board of education and the time he is to take the oath and enter upon the duties of his office. Such clerk shall also certify as soon as possible to the county superintendent of schools the persons so elected and their terms.

§ 193. (814.) VACANCIES, HOW FILLED.] The board of education of each city, town and village shall have power to appoint a person to fill any vacancy which may occur in the board; and such appointee shall hold his office until the next annual school election, at which time a person shall be elected to serve for the unexpired term; but if such vacancy shall occur within ten days before an annual election, such appointee shall hold office until the annual election in the following year. When any such appointment shall be made the clerk shall certify the same to the county superintendent.

§ 194. (815.) OATH OF OFFICE.] Before entering upon the duties of his office each person elected or appointed as a member of the board of education, shall take the oath or affirmation prescribed in section 211 of the constitution, which oath shall be filed with the clerk of the board.

§ 195. (816.) BONDS, HOW AND WHEN MAY BE ISSUED.] Whenever the taxes authorized by law shall not be sufficient or shall be deemed by the board of education to be burdensome, bonds may be issued and negotiated for the purpose of raising money to purchase a site or to erect suitable buildings thereon, or to fund any outstanding indebtedness of the school corporation; *provided*, that the issuance of such bonds shall first be authorized by the voters of such special district as hereinafter prescribed. Such bonds shall be signed by the president and clerk and attested by the corporate seal of the board, shall bear the date of their issue, and be payable in not less than five nor more than twenty years from their date, at such place as shall be designated upon their face; and such bonds shall be in denominations of not less than one hundred dollars, shall bear interest at not more than seven per cent per annum, payable semi-annually on the first day of January and July in each year, shall show upon their face that they are issued for school purposes, and shall be sold at not less than par. Each bond shall have indorsed thereon the certificate of the clerk of the board stating that such bond is issued pursuant to law and is within the debt limit prescribed by the constitution.

§ 196. (817.) ELECTION FOR ISSUING BONDS.] Before issuing any such bonds the board of education shall call an election for the purpose of submitting to the voters of the district the question of issuing such bonds, notice of which shall be given in the manner prescribed by law, for giving notice of the annual election for the several officers of the city, town or village comprising such special district, except that such notice shall be given twenty days before such election: Such election shall be conducted and the returns made in the manner provided for the annual election of members of the board of education, and may be held at the time of the annual school election or at any other time named in such notice. The notice of such election shall clearly state the amount of the bonds proposed to be issued, the time in which they shall be made payable, the purpose for which they are to be issued, and the time and place such election will be held. At such election the voters shall have written or printed on their ballots "for issuing bonds" or "against issuing bonds" and if a majority of the votes cast is for issuing bonds such bonds shall be issued and negotiated by such board of education, but if a majority thereof is against issuing bonds such bonds shall not be issued, nor shall the question be again submitted for one year thereafter except for a different amount and then only upon a written petition of a majority of the voters of the district.

§ 197. (818.) BONDS TO SPECIFY WHAT. DEBT LIMIT.] The bonds, the issuance of which is provided for in the foregoing section, shall specify the rate of interest and the time when the principal and interest shall be paid; and no district shall issue bonds in pursuance of this article in a sum greater than five per cent of its assessed valuation, including other debts.

§ 198 (819.) LEVY FOR INTEREST AND SINKING FUND.] The board of education at the time of its annual tax levy for the support of schools shall also levy a sufficient amount to pay the interest as the same accrues on all bonds issued under provisions of this article, and also to create a sinking fund for the redemption of such bonds, which it shall levy and collect in addition to the rate per cent authorized by the provisions aforesaid for school purposes, and such amount of funds when paid into the treasury shall be and remain a special fund for such purpose only and shall not be appropriated in any other way except as hereinafter provided. At or before the issuance of any bonds as herein provided the board shall by resolution provide for such annual levy to pay the interest and to create such sinking fund, and such resolution shall remain in force until all such bonds and the interest thereon shall have been paid.

§ 199. (820.) INVESTMENT OF SINKING FUND.] All moneys raised for the purpose of creating a sinking fund for the final redemption of all bonds issued under this article, shall be invested annually by the board of education in the bonds of this State or of the United States, or the board may buy and cancel the bonds of the district.

§ 200. (821.) INTEREST COUPONS.] When the interest coupons of the bonds hereinbefore authorized shall become due they shall be promptly paid, upon presentation, by the treasurer out of any moneys in his hands collected for that purpose, and he shall indorse in red ink upon the face of such coupons the word "paid" and the date of payment and sign the initials of his name.

§ 201. (822.) SECURITY FOR PAYMENT OF BONDS.] The school fund and property of such school corporation and territory attached for such purposes is hereby pledged to the payment of the interest and principal of the bonds mentioned in this article as the same may become due.

§ 202. (823.) BOND REGISTER.] The clerk of the board of education shall register in a book provided for that purpose the bonds issued under this article and all warrants issued by the board, which register shall show the number, date and amount of such bonds and to whom payable.

§ 203. (824.) REFUNDING BONDS, ISSUANCE OF.] The board of education of any special or independent school district shall have power, whenever two-thirds of the members of such board shall deem it necessary and for the best interests of such school district, to issue bonds for the purpose of refunding any outstanding bonds when the same become due. Such bonds shall not exceed in amount the face value of the bonds they are issued to replace, and shall not bear a higher rate of interest than seven per cent per annum, nor run for a longer period than twenty years.

§ 204. (825.) BONDS MAY BE EXCHANGED.] Such refunding bonds may be exchanged at par for an equal amount of outstanding bonds or may be sold at not less than par value and the proceeds applied solely to the payment of the bonds to be refunded, except that any premium that may be received on the sale of such bonds shall be kept as a separate fund and used for the payment of the interest on such bonds.

§ 205. (826.) ISSUE OF BONDS, HOW GOVERNED.] In the issuance of such refunding bonds the board of education shall be governed by the provisons of sections 818 to 823.

§ 206. (827.) SURPLUS FUNDS, HOW TRANSFERRED.] Any moneys remaining in the treasury of such school districts, appropriated or held for the purpose of paying such bonds so refunded, may, at the discretion of the board of education at any time within six months after such refunded bonds have been taken up and canceled, be transferred to the building or contingent fund of such district.

# ARTICLE XVIII.

## INDEPENDENT SCHOOL DISTRICTS.

Section.
207. Independent Districts, How Organized.
208. Notice of Election.
209. Form of Ballots—Returns.
210. Boundaries of Independent Districts.
211. Members of Board, How Elected—Quorum.
212. Date of Election—Canvass of Votes.
213. Vacancies, How Filled.
214. Style and Powers of Board.
215. Responsibility of Board.
216. Meetings of Board.
217. Secretary, Duties of.
218. Powers of Board.
219. Collection of Tax.
220. Amount of Tax Limited.
221. Authority to Issue Bonds.

Section.
222. Moneys Paid to City Treasurer.
223. Bond of Treasurer.
224. School Funds, How Kept and Paid Out.
225. General Powers of Board.
226. Visiting Schools.
227. Non-Resident Pupils.
228. Expenditures not to Exceed Revenues.
229. Title to Property of District.
230. Real Property—Title, How Conveyed.
231. Report of City Treasurer.
232. City Council to Pass Certain Ordinances.
233. Forfeit for Refusal to Serve as Member of Board.
234. New District to Assume Debts of Old.

§ 207. (828.) INDEPENDENT DISTRICTS, HOW ORGANIZED.] Any city heretofore organized for school purposes under a special law and provided with a board of education may become incorporated as an independent school district under the provisions of this article in the manner following: Whenever one-eighth of the legal voters of such city voting at the preceding municipal election shall petition the mayor and council thereof to submit the question as to whether such city shall establish an independent school district under this article to a vote of the electors in such city it shall be the duty of such mayor and council to submit such question accordingly and to appoint a time and place or places at which such vote may be taken and to designate the persons who shall act as judges at such election, but such question shall not be submitted oftener than once in two years.

§ 208. (829.) NOTICE OF ELECTION.] The mayor of such city shall cause at least twenty days' notice of such election to be given by publishing a notice thereof in one or more newspapers within such city, but if no newspaper is published therein, then by posting at least five copies of such notice in each ward or voting precinct.

§ 209. (830.) FORM OF BALLOTS. RETURNS.] The ballots to be used at such election shall be in the following form: "For establishing an independent school district" or "against establishing an independent school district." The judges of such election shall make returns thereof to the city council whose duty it shall be to canvass such returns and cause the result of such canvass to be entered upon the records of such city. If a majority of the votes cast at such election shall be for establishing an independent school district, such independent school district shall thenceforth be deemed to be organized under this article and the board of education then in office shall thereupon exercise the powers conferred upon like officers in this article until their successors are elected and qualified.

§ 210. (831.) BOUNDARIES OF INDEPENDENT DISTRICTS.] All that portion included within the corporate limits of any city together with the additions that are now or may be hereafter attached to such city limits shall be constituted and established an independent school district to be designated as the " Independent School District of the City of ........." and a board of education is hereby established for the same.

§ 211. (832.)  MEMBERS OF BOARD, HOW ELECTED.  QUORUM.] Such board shall consist of one member from each ward in the city, and when the city is divided into an even number of wards, then such city shall elect one member of such board at large. Such members shall hold their office for the term of two years and until their successors are elected and qualified.  A majority of the members of such board shall constitute a quorum for the transaction of business, but a smaller number may meet and adjourn.  The electors in each ward in such city shall elect one member of such board, and the electors of such city shall elect one member of the board at large.  The wards having even numbers shall hold their election in each even numbered year and the wards having odd numbers shall hold their election in each odd numbered year.  The member at large shall be elected biennially in the even numbered years.

§ 212. (833.)  DATE OF ELECTION.  CANVASS OF VOTES.]  The election referred to in the foregoing section shall be held on the third Monday in April of each year, at the usual polling place for municipal elections in each ward.  The mayor shall have authority and he is hereby empowered to appoint two judges and one clerk for such election, who shall open the polls at the hour of eleven o'clock in the forenoon and hold the same open until five o'clock in the afternoon of the same day.  Such election shall be conducted in all respects and the polls closed and votes canvassed in the same manner as municipal elections, and the judges shall have the same power and authority in all respects as the judges of election for municipal officers, and after the votes are canvassed the judges shall make their returns to the city clerk or auditor, as the case may be, within twenty-four hours after the polls are closed, and the city council shall canvass such returns and declare the result within three days thereafter, which result shall be entered upon the records of the city, and it shall be the duty of the city clerk or auditor to issue certificates of election to the persons declared elected.  The judges and clerks of election shall receive the same compensation for their services as at municipal elections for mayor and aldermen.

§ 213. (834.)  VACANCIES, HOW FILLED.  If any vacancy occurs in the board for any cause, the remaining members thereof shall fill such vacancy by appointment until the next annual election, and at such election a new member shall be elected to fill the unexpired term.

§ 214. (835.)  STYLE AND POWERS OF BOARD.]  The board so elected shall be a body corporate in relation to all the powers and duties conferred upon it by this article, and shall be styled

"The Board of Education of the Independent School District of the City of..........(here insert the name of the city)" and as such shall have power to sue and be sued, contract and be contracted with, and shall possess all the powers usual and incident to such bodies corporate, and as shall be herein given, and shall procure and keep a common seal. At each annual meeting of the board the members thereof shall elect one of their number president of the board, and when he is absent a president *pro tempore* shall be appointed who shall preside during such absence. The members so elected shall each qualify by taking the prescribed oath of office within ten days after receiving their certificate of election, and shall assume the duties of the office at the annual meeting of the board held on the first Monday in May of each year.

§ 215. (836.) RESPONSIBILITY OF BOARD.] The members of the board shall receive no compensation, nor be interested directly or indirectly in any contract for building or making any improvements or repairs provided by this chapter. They shall have the care and custody of all public property in such district pertaining to school purposes and the general management and control of all school matters.

§ 216. (837.) MEETINGS OF BOARD.] The regular meetings of the board shall be held on the first Tuesday of each month, and the board may hold special meetings upon notice. The regular meetings may be adjourned for any time shorter than one month. Special meetings may be called by the president, or in case of his absence or inability to act, by any three members of the board as often as necessary by giving a personal notice in writing to each member of the board or by causing such notice to be left at his place of residence at least forty-eight hours before the hour of such special meeting.

§ 217. (838.) SECRETARY, DUTIES OF.] Such board shall appoint a secretary who shall hold his office during the pleasure of the board and whose compensation shall be fixed by the board. The secretary shall keep a record of the proceedings of the board and perform such other duties as the board may prescribe. Such record or a transcript thereof, certified by the secretary and attested by the seal of the board, shall be received in all courts as *prima facie* evidence of the facts therein set forth; and such records, and all books, accounts, vouchers and papers of the board shall at all times be subject to inspection by the members of such board or any committee thereof, or by any taxpayer of the district. For the purpose of economy the board may, if deemed advisable, appoint one of its own members secretary. The annual report of the secretary shall contain such items as may be required by the Superintendent of Public Instruction.

§ 218. (839.) POWERS OF BOARD.] The board shall have power and it shall be its duty to levy and raise from time to time

by tax such sums as may be determined by the board to be necessary and proper for any of the following purposes:

1. To purchase, exchange, lease or improve sites for school
houses.

2. To build, purchase, lease, enlarge, alter, improve and repair
school houses and their outhouses and appurtenances.

3. To purchase, exchange, improve and repair school apparatus, books, furniture and appendages.

4. To procure fuel and defray the contingent expenses of the
board, including the expenses of the secretary.

5. To pay teachers' wages after the apportionment of public
moneys which may be by law appropriated and provided for that
purpose.

§ 219. (840.) COLLECTION OF TAX.] The tax to be levied
and collected as aforesaid by virtue of this article shall be collected in the same manner as other county taxes, and for that
purpose the board of education shall have power to levy and
cause to be collected such taxes as are herein authorized, and
shall cause the amount for each purpose to be certified by the
secretary to the county auditor in time to be added to and put
upon the annual tax list of the county. And it shall be the duty
of the county auditor to calculate and extend upon the annual
assessment roll and tax list the tax so levied by such board, and
such tax shall be collected as other county taxes are collected.

§ 220. (841.) AMOUNT OF TAX LIMITED.] The amount raised
for teachers' wages and contingent expenses shall be only such as
together with the public moneys coming to such district from
the State and county fund and other sources shall be sufficient to
maintain efficient and proper schools in such district. The taxes
for the purchasing, leasing or improving of sites, and the building,
purchasing, leasing, enlarging, altering or repairing of school
houses shall not exceed in any year twenty mills on the dollar
of the assessed valuation of the taxable property of the district,
and the board of education is authorized and directed, when
necessary, to borrow in anticipation, the amount of the taxes so
to be raised, levied and collected as aforesaid.

§ 221. (842.) AUTHORITY TO ISSUE BONDS.] The board of
education of such district is authorized and empowered and it is
its duty, whenever the board deems it necessary for the efficient
organization and establishment of schools in such district, and
when the taxes authorized by this article shall not be sufficient or
shall be deemed by the board to be burdensome upon the tax-
payers of the district, from time to time to issue bonds of the
district in the denomination of not less than one hundred dollars,
payable at a time not to exceed twenty-five years after date and
bearing interest at a rate not to exceed seven per cent per annum,
payable semi-annually, and upon their face to show that they are
issued for school purposes, and cause the same to be sold at not
less than par value and the money realized therefrom deposited

with the city treasurer to the credit of such board of education; and when any bonds shall be so negotiated it shall be the duty of the board to provide by tax for the payment of the principal and interest of such bonds; *provided*, that at no time shall the aggregate amount of such bonds exceed thirty mills on the dollar of valuation of the taxable property of such district to be determined by the last city assessment.

§ 222. (843.) MONEYS PAID TO CITY TREASURER.] All moneys raised pursuant to the provisions of this article and all moneys which shall by law be appropriated to or provided for such district, shall be paid over to the city treasurer of the city, and the county treasurer shall from time to time, as he shall receive the county school funds, and at least once in each month, on the first Monday thereof, pay over to such city treasurer the proportion thereof belonging to such district; and for that purpose the board shall have power to cause all needful steps to be taken, including census reports or other acts or things, to enable such board to receive the school money belonging to such district, as fully and completely as though such district formed one of the school districts of the county where the same may be situated.

§ 223. (844.) BOND OF TREASURER.] The city treasurer of such city shall give a bond to such board of education in such sum as the board shall from time to time require, with two or more sureties to be approved by the board, conditioned for the safe keeping of the school funds, which shall be in addition to his other bond; and such treasurer and the sureties upon such bond shall be accountable to the board for the moneys that come into his hands, and in case of failure of such treasurer to give such bond when required by the board, or within ten days thereafter, his office shall become vacant and the city council shall appoint another person in his place.

§ 224. (845.) SCHOOL FUNDS, HOW KEPT AND PAID OUT.] All moneys required to be raised by virtue of this article shall be paid in cash or in the warrants hereinafter provided, drawn on the school fund only, and such moneys and all moneys received by such district for the use of the common schools therein shall be deposited for safe-keeping with such city treasurer to the credit of the board of education and shall by him be safely kept separate and apart from any other funds until drawn from the treasury as herein provided. Such treasurer shall pay out the moneys authorized by this article only upon warrants drawn by the president, countersigned by the secretary and attested by the seal of such board of education.

§ 225. (846.) GENERAL POWERS OF BOARD.] The board shall have power and it shall be its duty:

1. To organize and establish such schools in the district as it shall deem requisite and expedient, and to change and discontinue the same.

2. To purchase, sell, exchange and hire school houses and rooms, lots or sites for school houses and to fence and improve the same.

3. To build, enlarge, alter, improve and repair school houses, outhouses and appurtenances as it may deem advisable upon lots and sites owned by the district.

4. To purchase, sell, exchange, improve and repair school apparatus, books for indigent pupils, furniture and appendages and provide fuel for schools.

5. To have the custody and safe keeping of the school houses, outhouses, books, furniture and appurtenances, and to see that the ordinances of the city council in relation thereto are observed.

6. To contract with and employ all teachers in such schools and to remove them at pleasure.

7. To pay the wages of such teachers out of the money appropriated and provided by law for the support of common schools in such district, so far as the same shall be sufficient, and the residue thereof from the money authorized to be raised by this article.

8. To defray the necessary and contingent expenses of the board, including the compensation of the secretary.

9. To have in all respects the superintendence, supervision and management of the common schools of such district, and from time to time to adopt, alter, modify and repeal, as they may deem expedient, rules and regulations for their organization, grading, government and instruction, for the reception of pupils and their transfer from one school to another, for the suspension and expulsion of pupils subject to the same restrictions as are contained in subdivision 11 of section 797, and generally for their good order, prosperity and utility.

10. To prepare and report to the city council of the city such ordinances and regulations as may be necessary and proper for their protection, safe keeping, care and preservation of school houses, lots, and sites and appurtenances and all the property belonging to the district connected with or appertaining to the schools within the city limits, and to suggest proper penalties for the violation of such ordinances and regulations, and annually, on or before the first Monday in July, to determine and certify to the county auditor the rate of taxation in its opinion necessary and proper to be levied under the provisions of this article for the year commencing on the first day of July thereafter, and also at any time to determine how many and what denomination of bonds shall be issued and sold to pay the extraordinary outlays required.

§ 226. (847.) VISITING SCHOOLS.] Each member of the board shall visit all the public schools in the district at least twice in each year of his official term, and the board shall provide that each of such schools shall be visited by a committee of three or more of their number at least once during such term.

§ 227. (848.) NONRESIDENT PUPILS.] Such board of education shall have power to allow the children not resident in such district to attend the schools of such district under the control and care of such board, upon such terms as the board shall prescribe, fixing the tuition which shall be paid therefor.

§ 228. (849.) EXPENDITURES NOT TO EXCEED REVENUES.] It shall be the duty of the board in all its expenditures and contracts to have reference to the amount of money which shall be subject to its order during the current year for the particular expenditures in question and not to exceed that amount.

§ 229. (850.) TITLE TO PROPERTY OF DISTRICT.] The title to all property belonging to any such independent school district shall be vested in such district for the use of the schools, and the same while used and appropriated for school purposes shall not be levied upon or sold by virtue of any warrant or execution or other process, nor be subject to any judgment or mechanic's lien or taxation for any purpose whatever; and the district in its corporate capacity may take, hold and dispose of any real and personal property transferred to it by gift, grant, bequest or devise for the use of common schools for the district, whether the same is transferred in terms to such district by its proper name or to any person or body for the use of such schools.

§ 230. (851.) REAL PROPERTY. TITLE, HOW CONVEYED.] Whenever any property is purchased by the board a conveyance thereof shall be taken in the name of such district; and whenever any sale of such property is made by the board a resolution in favor of such sale shall first be adopted and spread upon the records of the board, and the conveyance of such property shall be executed in the name of such district by the president of the board attested by the secretary under the seal thereof and acknowledged by such officers. Such president and secretary shall have authority to execute conveyances as aforesaid, with or without covenants of warranty on behalf of the district.

§ 231. (852.) REPORT OF CITY TREASURER.] It shall be the duty of the city treasurer at least fifteen days before the annual election for members of such board and as often as called upon by the board, to prepare and report to such board a true and correct statement of the receipts and disbursements of moneys under and pursuant to the provisions of this article, during the preceding year, which statement shall set forth under appropriate heads:

1. The money raised by the board under section 839.
2. The school moneys received from the county treasurer.
3. The money received under section 842.
4. All money received by the city treasurer, subject to the order of the board, specifying the sources from which it accrued.
5. The manner in which all money has been expended,

specifying the amount under each head of expenditures and the board shall at least one week before such election, cause such statement to be published in all the newspapers of the city which will publish the same gratuitously.

§ 232. (853.) CITY COUNCIL TO PASS CERTAIN ORDINANCES.] The city council shall have the power and it shall be its duty to pass such ordinances and regulations as the board of education may recommend as necessary for the protection, preservation, safe keeping and care of the school houses, lots, sites, appurtenances, libraries and all necessary property belonging to or connected with the schools of the city, and to provide proper penalties for the violation thereof; and all penalties shall be collected in the same manner that the penalties for the violation of city ordinances are collected, and when collected shall be paid to the city treasurer and placed to the credit of the board of education, and shall be subject to its order as herein provided.

§ 233. (854.) FORFEIT FOR REFUSAL TO SERVE AS MEMBER OF BOARD.] It shall be the duty of the clerk of such board immediately after the election of any person as a member thereof, personally or in writing to notify him of his election, and if any person shall not within ten days after receiving such notice of election, take and subscribe the oath as herein provided and file the same with the city auditor, the board may consider it as a refusal to serve, and fill the vacancy thus occasioned, and the person so refusing shall forfeit and pay to the city treasurer for the benefit of the schools of such district a penalty of fifty dollars, which may be recovered in the name of such city by a civil action.

§ 234. (855.) NEW DISTRICT TO ASSUME DEBTS OF OLD.] School districts created under the provisions of this article shall assume all obligations and liabilities incurred by the districts out of which they are formed, if old districts are not divided, and a proportionate part, if divided.

## ARTICLE XIX.

### BOARDS OF EDUCATION IN CERTAIN CITIES.

Section.
235. Boards to be Elected at Large.
236. Term of Office.
237. Elections, How Conducted.
238. Relatives Not Eligible as Teachers.
239. Independent School Organizations Under Special Laws Abolished.

Section.
240. Old School Officers Hold Over.
241. Debts and Assets Determined by Arbitration.

§ 235. (856.) BOARDS TO BE ELECTED AT LARGE.] In each city not organized under the general law there shall be a board of education consisting of seven members having the qualifications of electors who shall be elected at large by the electors of such city qualified to vote at school elections; and, except as may be otherwise provided herein for the first election, two members of such board shall be elected annually and three triennally at a special election to be held on the first Tuesday after the first Monday in June; *provided,* that the provisions of this article shall not apply to cities existing under a special act and which are now conducting their schools under the general school laws.

§ 236. (857.). TERM OF OFFICE.] The term of office of a member of the board of education, except as in this article otherwise provided, shall be three years and until his successor is elected and qualified.

§ 237. (858.) ELECTIONS, HOW CONDUCTED.] All elections under the provisions of this article shall be called, conducted and the votes canvassed and returned in the manner provided by law for general city elections.

§ 238. (859.) RELATIVES NOT ELIGIBLE AS TEACHERS.] No son, wife or daughter of any member of the school board shall be eligible to a position as teacher in schools of the district which such member represents, except upon the consent of all the members of such board.

§ 239. (860.) INDEPENDENT SCHOOL ORGANIZATIONS UNDER SPECIAL LAWS ABOLISHED.] Any independent district organized for school purposes under a special law, which does not include or is not included in any city or incorporated town or village organized for municipal purposes, shall become a part of the school district in which it is located by the repeal of the special law organizing or governing such independent district. Any independent district organized for school purposes under a special law or under any other law than is contained in this chapter, which includes or is included in any city or incorporated town or village organized for municipal purposes, shall become a special district by the repeal of the special law organizing or governing such independent school district. Any school district or special district so constituted or constituted in part shall be governed by the provisions of this chapter; *provided,* that nothing herein shall prevent any such independent district from coming under the operation of this chapter in the manner therein provided.

§ 240. (861.) OLD SCHOOL OFFICERS HOLD OVER.] The board of education or other governing board of such independent district shall continue to exercise the powers and duties devolving upon it under the provisions of such special or other law governing such independent district, the same as though such law had not been repealed, until the second Tuesday in July following the repeal of such special or other law; *provided,* that all that portion of the general school laws which provides for an annual school election shall apply to such independent district and shall be in full force and effect for the purpose of electing school officers at such annual school election; and such officers shall be elected in and for the whole school district, including the independent district or portion of such independent district located therein, or

S. L.—7.

in and for the special district, the same as though no law had ever existed providing for the organization of such independent district; *provided, further,* that in a special district formed and created as herein provided, a full board of education shall be elected as provided by law for first elections, but in school districts formed and created as herein provided by the addition of such independent district or portion thereof, there shall be elected only such officers as are required to fill the regular vacancies in the school offices of such school district heretofore organized.

§ 241. (862.) DEBTS AND ASSETS DETERMINED BY ARBITRATION.] When the boundaries of such school district shall have been arranged as contemplated in this article, the determination and division or consolidation of all debts, property and assets of the several portions of such district or districts so consolidated shall be made by arbitration as provided by law.

## ARTICLE XX.

### FREE TEXT BOOKS.

Section.                                          Section.
242. Power of School Boards.                      243. Proposition Submitted to Electors.

§ 242. (863.) POWER OF SCHOOL BOARDS.] The school board of any city, town or district in this State is hereby authorized and empowered to select, adopt or contract for the text books and other supplies needful for the use of the school or schools under its charge; and such board shall have power to purchase the text books selected or contracted for, and provide for the loan free of charge, or sale at cost, of such text books to the pupils in attendance at such school or schools as, provided for in the next section.

§ 243. (864.) PROPOSITION SUBMITTED TO ELECTORS.] Upon the petition of a majority of the qualified electors the school board of any city, town or district shall submit at the next annual school election to the legal voters thereof the question of providing free text books and other school supplies for the use of the pupils attending the schools under its charge. In case a majority of the legal voters present and voting shall vote in favor of free text books and other school supplies, the school board of such city, town or district so voting shall purchase, at the expense of such city, town or district, text books and other school supplies used in the public or common schools, and said text books and supplies shall be loaned to the pupils of said public schools free of charge, subject to such rules and regulations as to care and custody as the school board may prescribe.

# ARTICLE XXI.

## PURCHASE OF FLAGS FOR SCHOOL DISTRICTS.

Section.
244. United States Flag to be Displayed.

§ 244. (865.) UNITED STATES FLAG TO BE DISPLAYED.] The school board of each city, town and district is authorized and required to purchase at the expense of the city, town or district one or more flags of the United States, which shall be displayed upon the school houses or flagstaffs upon the school grounds during the school hours of each day's session of school.

# ARTICLE XXII.

## STATE EDUCATIONAL LIBRARY.

Section.
245. Appropriation for.

§ 245. (866.) APPROPRIATION FOR.] There is hereby appropriated out of any funds in the state treasury the sum of three hundred dollars annually, to be paid by warrant of the state auditor on the state treasurer upon the presentation of an itemized bill in due form by the Superintendent of Public Instruction, for the purchase of reference or pedagogical books for the State Educational Library in the office of such superintendent.

# ARTICLE XXIII.

## HIGH SCHOOL BOARD.

Section.
246. High School Board.
247. Students Classified.
248. Requirements for Classification.
249. School Visited Once Each Year.

Section.
250. No Compensation.
251. Discretionary Powers.
252. Shall Keep Record.

§ 246. (867.) HIGH SCHOOL BOARD.] The Governor, Superintendent of Public Instruction and President of the State University are hereby constituted a board of commissioners on preparatory schools for the encouragement of higher education in the State. Said board shall be called the " High School Board " and shall perform the duties and have and exercise the powers hereinafter mentioned.

§ 247. (868.) STUDENTS CLASSIFIED.] Any public graded school in any city or incorporated village or township organized into a district under the township or district system, which shall give instruction according to the terms and provisions of this article, and admit students of either sex from any part of the State, shall be entitled to be classified as a State High School; *provided, however,* that no such school shall be required to admit non-resident pupils unless they shall pass an examination in orthography, reading, penmanship, arithmetic, grammar, modern geography and United States history.

§ 248. (869.) REQUIREMENTS FOR CLASSIFICATION.] The board shall require of the schools desiring to be classified as State High Schools, compliance with the following requirements:

1. That there be regular and orderly courses of study, embracing all the branches prescribed by said board, for the first two years of the high school course.

2. That the schools classified as State High Schools under this article shall at all times permit the board of commissioners, or any member thereof, to visit and examine the classes pursuing such preparatory courses.

§ 249. (870.) SCHOOL VISITED ONCE EACH YEAR.] The board of commissioners shall cause each school classified as a State High School under this article to be visited, at least once in each school year, by a committee of one or more members, who shall carefully inspect the instruction and discipline of such high schools and make a written report on the same immediately; *provided*, that the board may, in its discretion, appoint in any case, competent persons to visit and inspect any schools and to make report thereon; and no school shall be classified as a State High School in any case until after such report shall have been received and examined by the board and the work of the school approved by a vote of the board.

§ 250. (871.) NO COMPENSATION.] The members of said board shall serve without compensation.

§ 251. (872.) DISCRETIONARY POWERS.] The high school board shall have full discretionary power to consider and act upon applications of schools for classification and to prescribe the conditions upon which such classification shall be made; and it shall be its duty to accept such schools only as will, in its opinion, if accepted, efficiently perform the service contemplated by law. Any school once accepted and continuing to comply with this article and with the regulations of the board made in pursuance thereof, shall be so classified not less than three years. The board shall have power to establish any necessary and suitable rules and regulations relating to examinations, reports, acceptance of schools, courses of studies, and other proceedings under this article.

§ 252. (873.) SHALL KEEP RECORD.] The board shall keep a careful record of all its proceedings and shall make on or before the first day of December in each year, a report, covering the previous school year, to the Superintendent of Public Instruction, showing the names and number of schools classified as State High Schools and the number of pupils attending the classes in each to which report it may add such recommendations as it may deem useful and proper.

# ARTICLE XXIV.

## HEALTH AND DECENCY IN PUBLIC SCHOOLS.

Section.
253. Duty of Boards of Education.

§ 253. (874.) DUTY OF BOARDS OF EDUCATION.] It shall be the duty of all boards of education and district school boards in this state to provide suitable and convenient water closets or privies for each of the schools under their charge, at least two in number, which shall be entirely separate each from the other, and having separate means of access; and it shall be the duty of the school officers aforesaid to keep the same in a clean, chaste and wholesome condition; and a failure to comply with the provisions of this article on the part of any board of education or district school board, shall be sufficient grounds for removal from office and for withholding from any district any part of the public moneys of the state. The expense incurred by the officers aforesaid in carrying out the requirements of this article shall be a charge upon the district, when such expense shall have been approved by the county superintendent of schools of the county within which the school district is located, and a tax may be levied therefor without a vote of the district.

# PART II.--EDUCATIONAL INSTITUTIONS.

## ARTICLE XXV.

### UNIVERSITY OF NORTH DAKOTA.

Section.
254. University, Where Located.
255. Board of Trustees to Govern.
256. Governor to Nominate—Vacancies, How Filled.
257. Powers and Duties of Board.
258. Meetings of the Board.
259. Number of Meetings Limited.
260. Government of University — Powers of Trustees.
261. Board May Expend Income.
262. Board to Make Report, When.
263. Powers of the President and Faculty.
264. Object and Departments of the University.
265. Courses of Instruction.
266. Scandinavian Language Taught.
267. Pupils, Who May Become.

Section.
268. Graduates Entitled to Certificates to Teach.
269. Tuition Fees.
270. Compensation of Trustees.
271. Trustees to Make Rules and By-Laws.
272. Salaries.
273. Secretary of State to Furnish Laws.
274. Supreme Court Reports, How Obtained.
275. Loan of Muskets Authorized.
276. Muskets, When Returned.
277. Geological Survey—Duty of Trustees.
278. Extent of the Survey.
279. Meteorological Statistics Tabulated.
280. Specimens Collected.
281. Map of the State.
282. Annual Report of Trustees.
283. State Geologist.

§ 254. (875.) UNIVERSITY, WHERE LOCATED.] The University of North Dakota as now established and located at the city of Grand Forks shall continue to be the university of the State.

§ 255. (876.) BOARD OF TRUSTEES TO GOVERN.] The government of such university shall be vested in a board of trustees consisting of five members to be appointed by the Governor by and with the advice and consent of the senate, who shall hold their office for the term of four years commencing on the first Tuesday in April next succeeding their appointment.

§ 256. (877.) GOVERNOR TO NOMINATE. VACANCIES, HOW FILLED.] The Governor shall nominate and, by and with the advice and consent of the senate, appoint during each regular session of the legislative assembly trustees of such university in the place of those whose terms shall thereafter first expire, and such trustees shall hold their office until their successors are appointed and qualified; *provided,* that the Governor shall fill any vacancy in such board by appointment to extend only until the first Tuesday in April succeeding the next regular session of the legislative assembly; and *provided, further,* that the Governor shall during such next regular session nominate and, by and with the advice and consent of the senate, appoint some person to fill such vacancy for the remainder of the term unexpired. Not more than two members of the board shall be appointed from the same county.

§ 257. (878.) POWERS AND DUTIES OF BOARD.] The board of trustees shall possess all the powers necessary to accomplish the objects and perform the duties prescribed by law, and shall have the custody of the books, records, buildings and all other property of such university. The board shall elect a president and a secretary who shall perform such duties as may be prescribed by the by-laws of the board. The secretary shall keep a correct record of all transactions of the board, and of the committees thereof, and in addition to performing the duties of secretary, he shall be the superintendent of the buildings and grounds of the university and discharge such other duties as may from time to time be prescribed by the board of trustees.

§ 258. (879.) MEETINGS OF THE BOARD.] The time for the election of the president and secretary of such board and the duration of their respective terms of office, the time for holding the regular annual meeting, and such other meetings as may be required, and the manner of giving notice of the same shall be determined by the board. Four members shall constitute a quorum for the transaction of business, but a less number may adjourn from time to time.

§ 259. (880.) NUMBER OF MEETINGS LIMITED.] Such board shall not hold more than twelve sessions in any year and such sessions shall not exceed twenty-four days in the aggregate; but the Governor may in his discretion authorize additional sessions.

§ 260. (881.) GOVERNMENT OF UNIVERSITY. POWERS OF TRUSTEES.] The board of trustees shall adopt rules for the government of the university in all its branches; elect a president and the requisite number of professors, instructors, officers and employees, fix the salaries and the term of office of each, and determine the moral and educational qualifications of applicants for admission to the various courses of instruction; but no instruction, either sectarian in religion or partisan in politics shall ever be allowed in any department of the university, and no sectarian or partisan test shall ever be allowed or exercised in the appointment of trustees, or in the election of professors, teachers or other officers of the university, or in the admission of students thereto or for any purpose whatever. Such board shall have power to remove the president or any professor, instructor or officer of the university, when in its judgment the interests of the university require it. The board may prescribe rules and regulations for the management of the library, cabinets, museum, laboratories and all other property of the university and of its several departments and for the care and preservation thereof, with suitable penalties and forfeitures by way of damages for their violation, which may be sued for and collected in the name of the board before any court having jurisdiction.

§ 261. (882.) BOARD MAY EXPEND INCOME.] The board is authorized to expend such portion of the income of the university fund as it may deem expedient for the erection of suitable buildings and the purchase of apparatus, a library, cabinets and additions thereto; and, if deemed expedient, it may unite with the

university as a branch thereof any college in the State, upon
application of its board of trustees; and such college so received
shall become a branch of the university and be subject to visitation by the trustees.

§ 262. (883.)  BOARD TO MAKE REPORT, WHEN.]  At the close
of each fiscal year the trustees through their president shall make
a report in detail to the governor, exhibiting the progress, condition and wants of each of the colleges embraced in the university,
the course of study in each, the number of professors and
students, the amount of receipts and disbursements, together with
the nature, cost and results of all important investigations and
experiments and such other information as they may deem
important, one copy of which shall be transmitted free by the
governor to each college endowed under the provisions of the
act of congress entitled "An act donating land to the several
states and territories which provide colleges for the benefit of
agriculture and mechanic arts," approved July 2, 1862, and also
one copy to the secretary of the interior.

§ 263. (884.)  POWERS OF THE PRESIDENT AND FACULTY.]
The president of the university shall be president of the several
faculties and the executive head of the instructional force in all
its departments; as such, he shall have authority, subject to the
power of the board of trustees to give general directions respect-
ing the instruction and scientific investigation of the several
colleges, and so long as the interests of the institution require it
he shall be charged with the duties of one of the professorships.
The immediate government of the several colleges shall be
intrusted to their respective faculties, but the trustees shall have
the power to regulate the course of instruction and prescribe the
books or works to be used in the several courses, and also to confer such degrees and grant such diplomas as are usual in universities, or as they shall deem appropriate, and to confer upon the
faculty, by by-laws, the power to suspend or expel students for
misconduct or other causes prescribed in such by-laws.

§ 264. (885.)  OBJECT AND DEPARTMENTS OF THE UNIVERSITY.]
The objects of the university shall be to provide the means of
acquiring a thorough knowledge of the various branches of learning connected with scientific, industrial and professional pursuits,
in the instruction and training of persons in the theory and art of
teaching, and also instruction in the fundamental laws of this
State and of the United States in regard to the rights and duties
of citizens, and to this end it shall consist of the following
branches or departments:

1.  The college or department of arts.
2.  The college or department of letters.
3.  The normal college or department.
4.  The school of mines, the object of which shall be to furnish
facilities for the education of such persons as may desire to

receive instruction in chemistry, metallurgy, mineralogy, geology, mining, milling and engineering.

5. The military department or school, the object of which shall be to instruct and train students in the manual of arms and such military maneuvers and tactics as are taught in military colleges.

6. Such professional or other colleges or departments as now are or may from time to time be added thereto or connected therewith, and the board of trustees is hereby authorized to establish such professional and other colleges or departments as in its judgment may be deemed necessary and proper; but no money shall be expended, by the board in establishing and organizing any of the additional colleges or departments provided for in this section, until an appropriation therefor shall have first been made.

§ 265. (886.) COURSES OF INSTRUCTION.] The college or department of arts shall embrace courses of instruction in mathematical, physical and natural sciences, with their application to industrial arts such as agricultural, mechanics, engineering, mining, and metallurgy, manufactures, architecture and commerce and such branches included in the college of letters as shall be necessary properly to fit the pupils in the scientific and practical courses for their chosen pursuits, and in military tactics; in the normal department, the proper instruction and learning in the theory and art of teaching and in all the various branches and subjects needful to qualify for teaching in the common schools; and as soon as the income of the university will allow, in such order as the wants of the public shall seem to require, the courses of sciences and their application to the practical arts shall be expanded into distinct colleges of the university, each with its own faculty and appropriate title. The college of letters shall be co-existent with the college of arts, and shall embrace a liberal course of instruction in languages, literature and philosophy, together with such courses or parts of courses in the college of arts as the trustees shall prescribe.

§ 266. (887.) SCANDINAVIAN LANGUAGE TAUGHT.] It shall be the duty of the trustees to cause to be taught at said institution the Scandinavian language, and for that purpose shall employ as one of the teachers of such institution a professor learned in that language.

§ 267. (888.) PUPILS, WHO MAY BECOME.] The university shall be open to students of both sexes under such regulations and restrictions as the board of trustees may deem proper, and all able bodied male students of the university may receive instruction and discipline in military tactics, the requisite arms for which shall be furnished by the State.

§ 268. (889.) GRADUATES ENTITLED TO CERTIFICATES TO TEACH.] After any person has graduated at the university, and after such graduation has successfully taught a public school in this State for sixteen months, the Superintendent of Public Instruction shall have authority and it shall be his duty to countersign the diploma of such teacher if upon examination he is satisfied that such person has a good moral character and is possessed of sufficient learning and ability to teach. Any person holding a diploma granted by the board of trustees of such university, certifying that the person holding the same has graduated from such university, shall, after his diploma has been countersigned by the Superintendent of Public Instruction as aforesaid, be deemed qualified to teach any of the public schools in the State, and such diploma shall be a certificate of such qualification until annulled by the Superintendent of Public Instruction.

§ 269. (890.) Tuition fees.] No student who shall have been a resident of the State for one year next preceding his admission shall be required to pay any fees for tuition in the university, except in the law department and for extra studies. The trustees may prescribe rates of tuition for any pupil in the law department, or who is not a resident as aforesaid, and for teaching extra studies.

§ 270. (891.) Compensation of trustees.] The trustees shall be entitled to receive the sum of three dollars per day for each day employed in attendance upon sessions of the board and all traveling expenses necessarily incurred thereby. Upon the presentation of the proper vouchers containing an itemized statement of the number of days attendance and money actually expended as above specified, duly verified by the oath of the trustee and certified by the president and secretary of the board, the State Auditor shall audit such claim and draw his warrant upon the State Treasurer for the amount allowed.

§ 271. (892.) Trustees to make rules and by-laws.] The board of trustees shall make rules, regulations and by-laws for the government and management of the university and of each department thereof. It shall also prescribe rules, regulations and by-laws for the admission of students; but each applicant for admission must undergo an examination to be prescribed by the board, and shall be rejected if it shall appear that he is not of good moral character. The board shall also require each applicant for admission in the normal department, other than such as shall, prior to admission, sign and file with such board a declaration of intention to follow the business of teaching in the common schools of this State for at least one year, to pay such fees for tuition as the board may deem proper and reasonable.

§ 272. (893.) Salaries.] The board of trustees shall from time to time fix the salary of the president, professors and teachers of such university, and shall certify the same to the State Auditor. Such board shall also from time to time certify to the State Auditor the amount due such persons for salary, and the

State Auditor shall draw his warrants upon the State Treasurer for the amounts so certified.

§ 273. (894.) SECRETARY OF STATE TO FURNISH LAWS.] The Secretary of State shall deliver to the university fifty copies of each volume of the general and special laws of the State, and the reports of the decisions of the supreme court, hereafter published, for use in the way of exchanges and otherwise in the establishment and maintenance of a law library for the law department of such university.

§ 274. (895.) SUPREME COURT REPORTS, HOW OBTAINED.] He shall procure for the purpose aforesaid from the publishers of the supreme court reports fifty copies of each volume thereof hereafter published, in addition to the number authorized for other purposes, to be paid for at the same price and in the same manner as such reports are delivered to the secretary for other purposes.

§ 275. (896.) LOAN OF MUSKETS AUTHORIZED.] The Adjutant General or whoever may be in charge of State arms shall, under the direction of the Governor, loan to the board of trustees of such university one hundred muskets and accoutrements or as many as can be spared, not exceeding that number, the same to be used for drill purposes by the students of such university.

§ 276. (897.) MUSKETS, WHEN RETURNED.] In case such arms and accoutrements are needed by the State at any time, the Governor or Adjutant General under his instructions may call in the same and the trustees of such university shall immediately turn the same over to such officer in good condition.

§ 277. (898.) GEOLOGICAL SURVEY. DUTY OF TRUSTEES.] It shall be the duty of the board of trustees of the university to cause to be begun as soon as may be practicable, and to carry on a thorough geological and natural history survey of the State.

§ 278. (899.) EXTENT OF THE SURVEY.] The geological survey shall be carried on with a view to a complete account of the mineral kingdom, as represented in the state, including the number, order, dip and magnitude of the several geological strata, their richness in ores, coals, clays, peats, salines and mineral waters, marls, cements, building stones and other useful materials, the value of said substances for economical purposes, and their accessibility; also an accurate chemical analysis of the various rocks, soils, ores, clays, peats, marls and other mineral substances of which a complete and exact record shall be made.

§ 279. (900.) METEOROLOGICAL STATISTICS TABULATED.] The board of trustees shall also cause to be collected and tabulated such meteorological statistics as may be needed to account for the varieties of climate in the various parts of the state; also to cause to be ascertained by barometrical observations or other appropriate means, the relative elevations and depressions of the different parts of the state; and also on or before the completion of such surveys to cause to be compiled from such actual surveys and measurements as may be necessary an accurate map of the

State; which map when approved by the Governor shall be the official map of the State.

§ 280. (901.) SPECIMENS COLLECTED.] It shall be the duty of-- said board to cause proper specimens, skillfully prepared, secured and labeled, of all rocks, soils, ores, coals, fossils, cements, building stones, plants, woods, skins and skeletons of animals, birds, insects and fishes, and other mineral, vegetable and animal substances and organisms discovered or examined in the course of said surveys, to be preserved for public inspection free of cost, in the University of North Dakota, in rooms convenient of access and properly warmed, lighted, ventilated and furnished, and in charge of a proper scientific curator; and they shall also, whenever the same may be practicable, cause duplicates in reasonable numbers and quantities of the above named specimens, to be collected and preserved for the purpose of exchange with other state universities and scientific institutions, of which latter the Smithsonian institution at Washington shall have the preference.

§ 281. (902.) MAP OF THE STATE.] The board shall cause a geological map of the state to be made as soon as may be practicable, upon which by colors and other appropriate means and devices the various geological formations shall be represented.

§ 282. (903.) ANNUAL REPORT OF TRUSTEES.] It shall be the duty of the board, through its president, to make on or before the second Tuesday in December of each year, a report showing the progress of said surveys, accompanied by such maps, drawings and specifications as may be necessary and proper to exemplify the same to the Governor, who shall lay the same before the legislative assembly, and the board upon the completion of any separate portion of any of the said surveys shall cause to be prepared a memoir or final report which shall embody in a convenient manner all useful and important information accumulated in the course of the investigation of the particular department or portion; which report or memoir shall likewise be communicated through the Governor to the legislative assembly.

§ 283. (904.) STATE GEOLOGIST.] The professor of geology in the university shall be *ex officio* State geologist.

# ARTICLE XXVI.

## NORMAL SCHOOLS.

Section.
284. Normal Schools Located.
285. Endowment and Maintenance.
286. Management of.
287. Boards, How Constituted.
288. Terms of Trustees.
289. Commissions.—Secretary.
290. Meetings.—Compensation.
291. Treasurer to Keep Funds.
292. Objects of Normal Schools.

Section.
293. Duties of Board as to Appropriations.
294. Salaries of Employees—Reports.
295. Salaries of Principal and Teachers.
296. The Faculty, Duties of.
297. Duty of Principal.
298. Annual Report of Faculty.
299. Biennial Reports to Governor.
300. Diplomas.
301. State Professional Certificate.

§ 284. (905.) NORMAL SCHOOLS LOCATED.] The normal school as established and located at the City of Mayville in the County of Traill, and the normal school as established and located at the City of Valley City in the County of Barnes, shall continue to be the normal schools of the State.

§ 285. (906.) ENDOWMENT AND MAINTENANCE.] All proceeds accumulating in the interest and income fund arising from the sale or rental of the lands granted or hereafter to be granted by the State of North Dakota, for such normal schools, are hereby pledged for the establishment and maintenance of such schools.

§ 286. (907.) MANAGEMENT OF.] The government and management of such schools are vested in a board of trustees to be known as the board of trustees of the State Normal Schools, and in a board of management for each school to be known as the board of management of the normal school at Mayville, and the board of management of the normal school at Valley City respectively.

§ 287. (908.) BOARDS, HOW CONSTITUTED.] The board of management for each normal school shall consist of five members. The board of trustees of such normal schools shall consist of twelve members, ten of whom shall be the members of the respective boards of management as herein provided. The Governor and Superintendent of Public Instruction shall be *ex officio* members of such board of trustees, and the Superintendent of Public Instruction shall act as president of such board.

§ 288. (909.) TERMS OF TRUSTEES.] The Governor shall by and with the advice and consent of the senate appoint during each biennial session of the legislative assembly, five members of such board of trustees who shall hold their office for four years commencing on the second Tuesday in April following such appointment. The Governor shall fill all vacancies therein by appointment for unexpired terms. At the first meeting of the board of management of each normal school the members thereof shall take and subscribe the oath of office required of all civil officers and shall proceed to elect a president who shall reside in the vicinity of such normal school, and the principal of the school shall be the secretary of the board but shall have no vote. In the absence of the principal the board may select one of its members to act as secretary. A majority of the members of the board of management shall constitute a quorum for the transaction of business.

§ 289. (910.) COMMISSIONS. SECRETARY.] The Governor shall cause to be issued to each of the members of the board of trustees a commission under the great seal of the state, and such commission shall designate the board of management upon which such members shall serve. At the first meeting of the board the members thereof shall proceed to select and appoint a secretary of the board. A majority of the members of the board of trustees shall constitute a quorum for the transaction of business.

§ 290. (911.) MEETINGS. COMPENSATION.] The board of trustees shall meet at Valley City and at Mayville or at the seat of government at such time each year as may be decided upon by the board. The members of the board shall receive their actual and necessary expenses in attending meetings of the board or in other duties connected therewith, which expenses shall be paid out of the State treasury upon the vouchers of the board approved by the State Auditor, who shall issue his warrant upon the State Treasurer for the amount so approved. The board of trustees shall not be in session for exceeding eight days in any one year nor either board of management to exceed twelve days during each year. The secretary of the board of trustees shall receive such salary as shall be determined by the board not exceeding one hundred dollars a year and his actual expenses incurred in attending meetings of the board, which shall be paid as herein provided for members of the board of trustees.

§ 291. (912.) TREASURER TO KEEP FUNDS.] All moneys arising from the interest and income derived from the rental and sale of the lands appropriated to such schools and all moneys that may hereafter be appropriated by the State, including all moneys raised in any other manner for either of such schools shall be deposited with the State Treasurer, to be by him kept in two separate funds, to be known as the fund of the State Normal School at Mayville, and the fund of the State Normal School at Valley City, respectively, and such funds shall be used exclusively for the benefit of such schools.

§ 292. (913.) OBJECTS OF NORMAL SCHOOLS.] The objects of such normal schools shall be to prepare teachers in the science of education and the art of teaching in public schools. The board of trustees, with the assistance of the respective faculties, shall adopt the full course of study prescribed for that purpose, which shall embrace the academic and professional studies usually taught in normal schools. Such schools shall in all things be free from sectarian control.

§ 293. (914.) DUTIES OF BOARD AS TO APPROPRIATIONS.] The board of management of each normal school shall direct the disposition of all moneys appropriated by the legislative assembly for current expenses for such school, and shall have supervision and charge of the construction of all buildings authorized by law for such school, and shall direct the disposition of all moneys appropriated therefor or accumulating therefor as provided in this article. They shall have power to appoint one of their members superintendent of construction of all buildings, who shall receive three dollars per day for each day actually and necessarily engaged in the discharge of his duties, not to exceed fifty days in any one year, which sum shall be paid out of the State treasury as herein provided; but all expenditures incurred under the direction of either of the boards aforesaid shall be audited and allowed by such board of management and the expenditures incurred under the direction of the board of trustees aforesaid shall be audited and allowed by such board.

§ 294. (915.) SALARIES OF EMPLOYEES. REPORTS.] The board of management of each normal school shall have the care of the buildings belonging to such school. It shall have power to fix the salaries of employees, except members of the faculty, and to prescribe their respective duties, and to remove any of such employees at any time. It shall at such times as may be deter-termined upon propose to the board of trustees the names of persons as principal, teachers and instructors, with tne recommendation that such persons be employed by such board of trustees as the faculty of such school. It shall on or before the third Monday in November of each year, make an annual report to the board of trustees, showing a statement of all expenditures of funds under its direction, the erection and care of buildings, the condition of the schools, and containing such recommendations as they may think proper.

§ 295. (916.) SALARIES OF PRINCIPAL AND TEACHERS.] The board of trustees shall fix the salaries of the principal, teachers and instructors, and shall employ the persons therefor that have been recommended by the respective boards of management, unless in the opinion of the board of trustees a reasonable ground exists for refusing to employ such person. The board of trustees shall prescribe the time and the length of the various terms of such schools.

§ 296. (917.) THE FACULTY, DUTIES OF.] The faculty shall consist of the principal, teachers and instructors employed for each school as herein provided. They shall pass all needful rules and regulations for the government and discipline of the schools, regulating the routine of labor, study, meals and the duties and exercises and such other rules and regulations as are necessary for the preservation of morals, decorum and health. They shall carry out the course of study adopted by the board of trustees and shall arrange for the classification of all pupils in conformity therewith.

§ 297. (918.) DUTY OF PRINCIPAL.] The principal shall be

the chief executive officer of the school and it shall be his duty to see that all the rules and regulations are executed. The subordinate officers and employees shall be under his direction and supervision.

§ 298. (919.) ANNUAL REPORT OF FACULTY.] The faculty shall, on or before the third Monday in October in each year make an annual report to the board of trustees showing the general condition of the school and containing such recommendations as the welfare of the institution demands.

§ 299. (920.) BIENNIAL REPORTS TO GOVERNOR.] The board of trustees shall make a report to the Governor on or before the fifteenth day of November next preceding each biennial session of the legislative assembly, containing the several reports of the boards of management and faculties herein provided for, showing the condition of the funds appropriated for the school, the money expended and the purpose for which the same was expended, in detail, and showing the condition of the normal schools generally.

§ 300. (921.) DIPLOMAS.] The board of trustees and the respective faculties of each school shall have power to issue diplomas to all persons who shall have completed the course of study prescribed for the normal schools as herein provided, and who shall have passed a satisfactory examination under the direction of the board of trustees, upon the branches contained in such course, and who shall be known to possess a good moral character, which diploma shall set forth the above mentioned facts and shall be designated the State Normal School diploma.

§ 301. (922.) STATE PROFESSIONAL CERTIFICATE.] Any person who is the holder of such a diploma and who can furnish satisfactory evidence to the Superintendent of Public Instruction that he has had three years' successful experience as a teacher, shall be granted by the Superintendent of Public Instruction a State professional certificate, valid for life, as provided by law, and any such person who can furnish satisfactory evidence of one year's successful experience as a teacher shall be granted such certificate, valid for five years, as provided by law. The fees for such certificate shall be as provided by law.

# ARTICLE XXVII.

## NORTH DAKOTA ACADEMY OF SCIENCE.

Section.
302. Academy of Science, Location of.
303. Management
304. Board, How Appointed.
305. Powers of Board.
306. Rules and Regulations.
307. Official School Visits.
308. Expenses of Board How Paid—Faculty, How Paid.

Section.
309. Appropriation for Construction and Maintenance.
310. Temporary Funds, How Secured—Certificates Issued.
311. State Treasurer Custodian of all Funds.
312. Record and Proceedings of Board.

§ 302. (923.) ACADEMY OF SCIENCE, LOCATION OF.] The North Dakota Academy of Science heretofore established at Wahpeton is hereby continued as such. The object of such academy shall be to furnish instruction in such arts and sciences as the board of trustees shall prescribe. Such academy shall contain a preparatory department where all the various branches shall be taught pertaining to a good common school education.

§ 303. (924.) MANAGEMENT.] Such school shall be under the direction of a board of trustees and shall be governed and supported as hereinafter provided.

§ 304. (925.) BOARD, HOW APPOINTED.] Such board shall consist of five members, three of whom shall be appointed by the Governor as follows: During each biennial session of the legislative assembly the Governor shall nominate and, by and with the advice and consent of the senate, appoint one member of such board who shall hold his office for the period of six years, commencing on the first Tuesday in April succeeding such appointment, and until his successor is appointed and qualified and the Governor may fill vacancies in such board by appointment as in other cases. The State Treasurer and Superintendent of Public Instruction shall be *ex officio* members of such board; and the members thereof shall annually elect from their number a president and secretary. It shall be the duty of the secretary to keep a detailed account of the acts of the board, and he shall make such reports to the legislative assembly as are required by this article.

§ 305. (926.) POWERS OF BOARD.] Such board shall have power to appoint a principal and assistant to take charge of such school, and such other teachers and officers as may be required and fix the salaries of each, and prescribe their several duties. It shall also have power to remove either the principal, assistant or teachers and appoint others in their stead. The board shall prescribe the various books to be used in such school and shall make all the regulations and by-laws necessary for the good government and management of the same, and shall have power to procure all necessary apparatus, instruments and appurtenances for instruction in such schools.

S. L.—8.

§ 306. (927.) RULES AND REGULATIONS.] The board shall prescribe such rules and regulations for the admission of pupils to said school as it shall deem necessary and proper. Each applicant for admission shall undergo an examination in such manner as shall be prescribed by the board. And the board may in its discretion require applicants for admission into such school to pay or secure to be paid such fees or tuition as the board shall deem reasonable.

§ 307. (928.) OFFICIAL SCHOOL VISITS.] There shall be appointed annually by the board three persons, not members of such board, whose duty it shall be to visit such school at least once in each year and report to the Superintendent of Public Instruction their views in regard to its condition, success and usefulness, and any other matters which they may deem expedient.

§ 308. (929.) EXPENSES OF BOARD, HOW PAID. FACULTY, HOW PAID.] All necessary expenses incurred by members of the board of trustees under the provisions of this article shall be paid on the proper voucher out of any funds belonging to such institution n the hands of the State Treasurer, but they shall receive no other compensation. The principal, assistant, teachers, board of trustees and other officers employed in such school shall be paid out of the fund of the North Dakota Academy of Science.

§ 309. (930.) APPROPRIATION FOR CONSTRUCTION AND MAINTENANCE.] All moneys received from the interest and income derived from the sale or leasing of the forty thousand acres of land donated by congress and appropriated by the constitution of the State for the benefit of such school, are hereby appropriated for the construction and maintenance thereof.

§ 310. (931.) TEMPORARY FUNDS, HOW SECURED. CERTIFICATES ISSUED.] To provide temporarily for the erection and maintenance of such academy the board of trustees may receive such sums of money as can be actually used in the construction of permanent buildings, procuring ground whereon to build the same, and other needed and necessary improvements to be made and expenses incurred in connection therewith, not exceeding the sum of ten thousand dollars, and to each person, association, or corporation so subscribing and advancing money as aforesaid, the board shall issue a certificate stating the date of issue and the amount of subscription, which certificate shall bear interest at not exceeding six per cent per annum and shall be made payable from the funds to accumulate in the interest and income fund arising from interest on the permanent fund or from rents received for any lands set apart for such academy, or from any appropriation that may hereafter be made for that purpose; *provided*, that until a sufficient amount of money accumulates in the fund provided for that purpose, with which to pay such certificates, the holders thereof shall each be paid a pro rata share of all moneys to be paid on such indebtedness; *provided, further*, that no part of any appropriation hereafter to be made from the State treasury, unless specifically appropriated for that purpose, shall ever be used in payment of such indebtedness or any part thereof.

§ 311. (932.) STATE TREASURER CUSTODIAN OF ALL FUNDS.] All money that may arise from the interest received and all money derived from the sale of lands heretofore or that may hereafter be appropriated for such academy, including all money that may be received from the rents of such lands, and all moneys that may be hereafter appropriated for such academy by this state, including all money raised in any other manner or donated to said academy, shall be deposited with the State Treasurer to be by him kept in a separate fund which shall be known as the North Dakota Academy of Science fund and shall be used exclusively for the benefit of such academy.

§ 312. (933.) RECORD AND PROCEEDINGS OF BOARD.] A majority of the members of such board shall constitute a quorum for the transaction of business, but a less number may adjourn from time to time. All proceedings of the board shall be recorded in a book to be kept for that purpose, which shall be open to inspection by any person on request.

## ARTICLE XXVIII.

### AGRICULTURAL COLLEGE.

Section.
313. Location of.
314. Management of.
315. Board of Trustees, How Appointed—Vacancies.
316. Commission—Oath—Organization.
317. Meetings, Where Held.
318. Duties of Board.
319. Course of Instruction.
320. Board of Trustees to Fix Salaries.

Section.
321. Faculty to Adopt Rules and Regulations.
322. Duties of President.
323. Faculty to Make Annual Report to Board.
324. Annual Report to Governor.
325. Honorary Degrees May be Conferred.
326. Experiment Station
327. Legislative Assent to Grant by Congress.
328. Acceptance of Land Grant.
329. Bond of Treasurer.

§ 313. (934.) LOCATION OF.] The Agricultural College shall continue as now established and located at Fargo in the county of Cass.

§ 314. (935.) MANAGEMENT OF.] The government and management of such college is vested in a board of trustees to be known as the board of trustees of the Agricultural College.

§ 315. (936.) BOARD OF TRUSTEES, HOW APPOINTED. VACANCIES.] The board of trustees shall consist of seven members, to be appointed as follows: During each biennial session of the legislative assembly there shall be nominated by the Governor and, by and with the advice and consent of the senate, appointed for the term of four years, trustees to fill vacancies occurring by the expiration of the term of office of those previously appointed. The Governor shall have power to fill all vacancies in such board which occur when the legislative assembly is not in session, and the members of such board shall hold their office until their successors are appointed and qualified as provided in this article,

Persons appointed to fill vacancies shall hold office only until the first Tuesday in April succeeding the next session of the legislative assembly.

§ 316. (937.) COMMISSION. OATH. ORGANIZATION.] The Governor shall cause to be issued to each trustee so appointed a commission under the great seal of the State. At the first meeting of such board the members thereof shall take and subscribe the oath of office required of other civil officers and shall then proceed to elect a president, secretary and treasurer, but the treasurer shall not be a member of the board. A majority of the members of the board shall constitute a quorum for the transaction of business. The board shall require a bond of its treasurer in such an amount and with such sureties as it may deem proper.

§ 317. (938.) MEETINGS, WHERE HELD. COMPENSATION OF TRUSTEES.] The board shall hold its meetings at the city of Fargo at such times as it may designate, but there shall not be to exceed six regular meetings each year; *provided*, that the president of the board shall have power to call special meetings whenever in his judgment it becomes necessary. The members of the board shall receive as compensation for their services the sum of three dollars per day for each day employed and five cents per mile for each mile actually and necessarily traveled in attending the meetings of the board, which sum shall be paid out of the State treasury upon vouchers of the board duly certified by the president and secretary thereof.

§ 318. (939.) DUTIES OF BOARD.] Such board shall direct the disposition of all moneys appropriated by the legislative assembly or by the congress of the United States, or that may be derived from the sale of lands donated by congress to the State for such college, or that may be donated to or come from any source to the State for said college, or experiment station for North Dakota, subject to all restrictions imposed upon such funds either by the constitution or laws of the State or by the terms of such grants from congress, and shall have supervision and charge of the construction of all buildings authorized by law for such college and station. The board shall have power to employ a president and necessary teachers, instructors and assistants to conduct such school and carry on the experiment station connected therewith and to appoint one of its members superintendent of construction of all buildings, who shall receive three dollars per day for each day actually and necessarily engaged in the discharge of his duties, not to exceed fifty days in any one year, which sum shall be paid out of the State treasury upon the vouchers of said board.

§ 319. (940.) COURSE OF INSTRUCTION.] The object of such college shall be to afford practical instruction in agriculture and the natural sciences connected therewith, and in the sciences which bear directly upon all industral arts and pursuits. The course of instruction shall embrace the English language and literature, mathematics, military tactics, civil engineering, agricultural chemistry, animal and vegetable anatomy and physiology, the veterinary art, entomology, geology and such other natural sciences as may be prescribed, political, rural and household economy, horticulture, moral philosophy, history, book-keeping and especially the application of science and the mechanic arts to practical agriculture. A full course of study in the institution shall embrace not less than four years, and the college year shall consist of not less than nine calendar months, which may be divided into terms by the board of trustees as in its judgment will best secure the objects for which the college was founded.

§ 320. (941.) BOARD OF TRUSTEES TO FIX SALARIES.] The board of trustees shall fix the salaries of the president, teachers, instructors and other employees and prescribe their respective duties. The board shall also fix the rate of wages to be allowed the students for labor on the farm and experiment station or in the shops or kitchen of the college. The board may remove the president or subordinate officers and supply all vacancies.

§ 321. (942.) FACULTY TO ADOPT RULES AND REGULATIONS.] The faculty shall consist of the president, teachers and instructors and shall pass all needful rules and regulations for the government and discipline of the college, regulating the routine of labor, study, meals and the duties and exercises, and all such rules and regulations as are necessary for the preservation of morals, decorum and health.

§ 322. (943.) DUTIES OF PRESIDENT.] The president shall be the chief executive officer of the college and it shall be his duty to see that all rules and regulations are executed, and the subordinate officers and employees not members of the faculty shall be under his direction and supervision.

§ 323. (944.) FACULTY TO MAKE ANNUAL REPORT TO BOARD.] The faculty shall make an annual report to the board of trustees on or before the first Monday in November of each year, showing the condition of the school, experiment station and farm and the results of farm experiments and containing such recommendations as the welfare of the institution demands.

§ 324. (945.) ANNUAL REPORT TO GOVERNOR.] The board of trustees shall on or before the fifteenth day of November in each year make a report to the Governor setting forth in detail the operations of the experiment station, including a statement of the receipts and expenditures, a copy of which report shall be sent by the Governor to the Commissioner of Agriculture and to the Secretary of the Treasury of the United States, and the board shall also make a report to the Governor on or before the fifteenth day of November next preceding each biennial session of the legislative assembly, containing a financial statement showing the condition of all funds appropriated for the use of such college and experiment station, also the moneys expended and the purposes for which the same were expended, in detail, also the condition of the institution and the results of the experiments carried on there.

§ 325. (946.) HONORARY DEGREES MAY BE CONFERRED.] The board and the faculty shall have power to confer degrees upon all persons who shall have completed the course of study prescribed by them, and who shall have passed a satisfactory examination in the branches contained in such course, and who possess a good moral character.

§ 326. (947.) EXPERIMENT STATION.] The agricultural experiment station, heretofore established in connection with such college is continued and the same shall be under the direction of the board of trustees of such college, for the purpose of conducting experiments in agriculture according to the provisions of section 1 of the act of congress approved March 2, 1887, entitled "An act to estabish agricultural experiment stations in connection with the colleges established in the several states under the provisions of an act approved July 2, 1862, and of the acts supplementary thereto."

§ 327. (948.) LEGISLATIVE ASSENT TO GRANT BY CONGRESS.] The assent of the legislative assembly is hereby given in pursuance of the requirements of section 9 of said act of congress, approved March 2, 1887, to the grant of money therein made and to the establishing of an experiment station in accordance with section 1 of said last mentioned act, and assent is hereby given to carry out the provisions of said act.

§ 328. (949.) ACCEPTANCE OF LAND GRANT.] The grants of land accruing to this State by virtue of an act of congress donating public lands for the use and support of agricultural colleges, approved February 22, 1889, is hereby accepted with all the conditions and provisions in said act contained, and said lands are hereby set apart for the use and support of the colleges herein provided for.

§ 329. (950.) BOND OF TREASURER.] The treasurer of such college shall give a bond in the sum of fifty thousand dollars with at least four sureties to be approved by the board of trustees of such college, conditioned for the faithful accounting of all moneys received by him as such treasurer.

## ARTICLE XXIX.

### DEAF AND DUMB ASYLUM.

Section.
330. Location.
331. Board of Trustees, How Appointed.
332. Organization—Meetings.
333. Oath—Duties of Officers of Board.
334. Board to Direct Disposition of Moneys.
335. Duties of Board.
336. Indebtedness Limited.
337. Compensation of Members of Board.
338. Fee for Non-Resident Children.

Section.
339. Residents Entitled to Education Free.
340. Deaf to be Reported to Principal of School.
341. Accounts for Clothing, How Collected.
342. Transportation of Indigent Persons, How Paid.
343. Faculty—Duties of Principal.
344. Duty of Matron.
345. Board to Make Biennial Reports.

§ 330. (951.) LOCATION.] The deaf and dumb asylum as located by the constitution at Devils Lake shall continue to be the institution for the support and education of the deaf and dumb children of the State.

§ 331. (952.) BOARD OF TRUSTEES, HOW APPOINTED.] Such institution shall be under the supervision of a board of trustees consisting of five members, who shall be appointed by the Governor by and with the advice and consent of the senate. At each biennial session of the legislative assembly the Governor shall nominate and, by and with the advice and consent of the senate, appoint for the term of four years, trustees to fill vacancies occurring by the expiration of the term of office of those previously appointed, and the Governor shall have power to fill all vacancies in the board which occur when the legislative assembly is not in session, and the members of such board shall hold their office for the term of four years commencing on the first Tuesday in April succeeding their appointment, and until their successors are appointed and qualified, except members appointed to fill vacancies during the recess of the legislative assembly, which members shall hold only until the first Tuesday in April succeeding the next regular session of the legislative assembly.

§ 332. (953.) ORGANIZATION. MEETINGS.] Such trustees shall meet in the City of Devils Lake. They shall choose from among their number a president and secretary, who shall hold office for two years, and until their successors are appointed and qualified. Three members of the board shall constitute a quorum for the transaction of business. Such board shall meet annually in the month of April and as often thereafter as may be deemed necessary for the proper transaction of business, upon the call of the president or secretary.

§ 333. (954.) OATH. DUTIES OF OFFICERS OF BOARD.] Each member of the board shall before entering upon his duties take and subscribe the oath required of other civil officers, which oath shall be filed in the office of the Secretary of State. The president shall preside at all meetings of the board when present and in his absence a president *pro tempore* may be named to perform the duties of president. The secretary shall keep a correct record of the proceedings of the board and have charge, in trust for the institution, of all papers and records of the same.

§ 334. (955.) BOARD TO DIRECT DISPOSITION OF MONEYS.] The board shall direct the disposition of all moneys appropriated by the legislative assembly or received from any other source for the benefit of such institution.

§ 335. (956.) DUTIES OF BOARD.] Such board shall have general supervision of the institution, adopt rules for the government thereof, employ and fix the salaries of all employees, provide necessaries for the institution and perform other duties, not devolving upon the principal, necessary to render it efficient and to carry out the provisions of this article.

§ 336. (957.) INDEBTEDNESS LIMITED.] The board shall not create any indebtedness against such institution exceeding the amount appropriated by the legislative assembly for the use thereof.

§ 337. (958.) COMPENSATION OF MEMBERS OF BOARD.] The members of the board shall receive as compensation for their services three dollars per day for each day employed, and five cents per mile for each mile actually and necessarily traveled in attending meetings of the board, to be paid out of the State treasury upon vouchers of the board duly certified by the president and secretary thereof.

§ 338. (959.) FEE FOR NONRESIDENT CHILDREN.] Deaf and dumb children, not residents of this State, of suitable age and capacity, shall be entitled to an education in such school on payment to the State Treasurer of the sum of one hundred and eighty dollars per annum, in advance, but such children shall not be received to the exclusion of children of this State.

§ 339. (960.) RESIDENTS ENTITLED TO EDUCATION FREE.] Each deaf and dumb person, who is a resident of this State, of suitable age and capacity, shall be entitled to receive an education in such institution at the expense of the State.

§ 340. (961.) DEAF TO BE REPORTED TO PRINCIPAL OF SCHOOL.] The assessors in each county shall annually report to the county auditor the names, ages, post office address and names of parents or guardian of each deaf and dumb person between the ages of five and twenty-five years residing in his district, including all such persons as may be too deaf to acquire an education in the common schools. Such county auditor shall, on or before the first day of August in each year, send a list containing the names, ages and residences of all such persons to the principal of the school.                    •

§ 341. (962.) ACCOUNTS FOR CLOTHING, HOW COLLECTED.] When the pupils of such institution are not otherwise provided or supplied with suitable clothing, they shall be furnished therewith by the principal, who shall make out an account thereof in each case against the parent or the guardian, if the pupil is a minor, and against the pupil if he has no parent or guardian or if he has attained the age of majority; which account shall be certified to be correct by the principal, and when so certified such account shall be presumed correct in all courts. The principal shall thereupon transmit such account by mail to the county treasurer of the county from which the pupil so supplied shall have come; and such treasurer shall proceed at once to collect the amount by suit in the name of his county, if necessary, and pay the same into the State treasury. The principal shall at the same time remit a duplicate of such account to the State Auditor, who shall credit the same to the account of the school and charge it to the proper county; *provided*, that if it shall appear by the affidavit of three disinterested citizens of the county, not of kin to the pupil, that such pupil or his parents would be unreasonably oppressed by such suit, then such treasurer shall not commence such action, but shall credit the same to the State on his books and report the amount of such account to the board of county commissioners of his county, which board shall levy a sufficient tax to pay the same to the State and cause the same to be paid into the State treasury.

§ 342. (963.) TRANSPORTATION OF INDIGENT PERSONS, HOW PAID.] The board of county commissioners shall order to be paid the expenses of transportation to and from such institution of any indigent deaf and dumb children entitled to admission thereto, and they shall at the time of levying other taxes, levy a tax sufficient to reimburse the county therefor. In order to avoid long delay in transporting indigent children to and from the institution, the principal may, upon correspondence with the auditor of such county, pay such transportation and forward to such county auditor an itemized statement of the expenses. The board of county commissioners shall order the county treasurer to draw his warrants for such amount in favor of the principal of the institution, who shall account for such money as provided by law.

§ 343. (964.) FACULTY. DUTIES OF PRINCIPAL.] The officers of the institution shall be a principal and a matron. The principal shall be a capable person, skilled in the sign language and all the methods in use in educating the deaf and shall have knowledge of the wants and requirements of the deaf in their proper training and instruction. The principal and matron must reside at the institution. The principal shall receive a salary of not less than fifteen hundred dollars per annum. The principal shall annually make to the board of trustees a written report stating in full the true condition of the educational, the domestic and the industrial departments of the institution and his action and proceedings therein, which report shall be embraced in the report of the trustees to the Governor. He shall keep and have charge of all necessary records and registers of each department and have the supervision of teachers, pupils and servants and perform such other duties as the board may require. He may recommend and with the approval of the board employ all assistants needed therein. He shall have special charge of the male pupils, out of school hours, and shall furnish them with employment about the premises or in some trade to which they are adapted when such trades have been organized and established at the institution by the trustees and provision for their maintenance made by the legislative assembly. The proceeds and products arising from the labor and employment of the pupils shall inure to the use and benefit of the institution.

§ 344. (965.) DUTY OF MATRON.] The matron of the school shall have control of the internal arrangement and management of the institution and of the female pupils, out of school hours. She shall instruct the female pupils in the domestic arts or in some trade to which they are adapted, under the direction of the principal.

§ 345. (966.) BOARD TO MAKE BIENNIAL REPORTS.] The board of trustees shall on or before the fifteenth day of November preceding each regular session of the legislative assembly make a full and complete report to the Governor, showing:

1. A statement of the financial condition of the institution from the date of the last report, giving in detail the amount of moneys received from all sources and the amount expended.

2. The value of real estate and buildings at the date of the last report and the cost of improvements made, if any, since such report.

3. The number of pupils in attendance, their names, ages, residences, and cause of deafness; also the number that have entered the institution, and the number of those who have left since the last report.

4. The number and cause of deaths if any, which have occurred in the institution since the last report.

5. The improvement, health and discipline of the pupils.

6. The names of the officers, teachers and servants employed.

7. All other needful information touching such matters as may be deemed of interest.

8. Such recommendations as may be deemed needful.

# ARTICLE XXX.

### BLIND ASYLUM.

Section.
346. Location and Government.
347. Trustees, How Appointed — Length of Term.
348. Organization of Board—Quorum.

Section.
349. Meetings of Board—Compensation.
350. Proceeds from Land Grant.
351. By-Laws and Rules of Regulation.
352. Reports, When Made.

§ 346. (967.) LOCATION AND GOVERNMENT. There is hereby established and located at Bathgate in Pembina county, a blind asylum, which shall be known by the name of the North Dakota

Blind Asylum. The government and management of said asylum is hereby vested in a board of trustees consisting of five members, which shall be styled the board of trustees of the North Dakota Blind Asylum.

§ 347. (968.) TRUSTEES, HOW APPOINTED. LENGTH OF TERM.] The members of the board shall be nominated by the Governor, and, by and with the advice and consent of the senate, shall be appointed on or before the third Monday of February of each biennial session of the legislative assembly, for a period of four years from said date; *provided, however*, that the first board of trustees shall be appointed by the Governor at once upon the taking effect of this act; and *provided, further*, that the terms of the first board shall be, three members for the period of four years, and two members for the period of two years, the length of the term of the respective trustees to be designated by the Governor in making the appointments. Such appointments shall be made by and with the advice and consent of the senate, when the legislative assembly is in session; otherwise the trustees appointed shall qualify and hold office until their successors are appointed and qualified. The Governor shall have power to fill all vacancies which may occur in said board when the legislative assembly is not in session, and the members of said board shall hold their office until their successors are appointed and qualified as provided herein.

§ 348. (969.) ORGANIZATION OF BOARD. QUORUM.] The Governor shall cause to be issued to each of said trustees a commission, which shall be under the great seal of the State. At the first meeting of said board the members thereof shall take and subscribe the oath of office required of all civil officers and shall then proceed to elect a president, secretary and treasurer, but the treasurer need not be a member of the board. A majority of the trustees shall constitute a quorum for the transaction of business. The board shall require a bond of its treasurer and fix the amount thereof.

§ 349. (970.) MEETINGS OF BOARD. COMPENSATION.] The board shall hold its meetings at Bathgate and fix the time of holding the same; *provided*, there shall not be to exceed twelve regular meetings in each year. The members of the board shall receive as compensation for their services three dollars per day for each day employed, not to exceed twenty-four days in any one year, and five cents per mile for each mile actually and necessarily traveled in attending the meetings of the board, which sum shall be paid out of the State treasury on the vouchers of said board; *provided*, that until such time as the legislative assembly shall make an appropriation for the construction and maintenance of such asylum, or until there shall be derived from the interest on the proceeds of sales of or rents derived from the thirty thousand acres appropriated for this asylum, sufficient funds to construct and maintain such asylum, the sum of five thousand dollars, the trustees appointed under this act shall receive no compensation whatever, nor shall they issue their warrant upon the State treasury for any purpose whatever.

§ 350. (971.) Proceeds from land grant.] The thirty thousand acres of land donated by congress for the purpose of such blind asylum and appropriated by the constitution of this State therefor, and all moneys received from the interest and income derived from the sales of such lands or rents derived from the leasing of such lands, are hereby appropriated for the construction and maintenance of said asylum.

§ 351. (972.) By-laws and rules of regulation.] The board shall direct the disposition of all moneys appropriated by the legislative assembly or the interest on all moneys that may be derived from the sale, or the rent derived from the leasing of land donated by congress to this State and by the constitution of the State appropriated for such asylum, and shall have supervision and charge of the construction of all buildings provided for or authorized by law for said asylum. Said board shall have power to enact by-laws and rules for the regulation of all its concerns not inconsistent with the laws of this State, to see that its affairs are conducted in accordance with the requirements of law; to provide employment and instruction for the inmates; to appoint a superintendent, a steward, a matron, a teacher or teachers, and such other officers as in its judgment the wants of the institution may require, and prescribe their duties; to exercise a general supervision over the institution, its officers and inmates, fix the salaries to be paid to the officers and to order their removal, upon good cause.

§ 352. (973.) Reports, when made.] The board shall make a report to the Governor on or before the last Monday in December next preceding each biennal session of the legislative assembly, containing a financial statement showing the condition of all funds appropriated for the asylum; also the money expended and the purpose for which the same was expended in detail; also showing the condition of the institution generally.

## ARTICLE XXXI.

### INDUSTRIAL SCHOOL.

Section.
353. Location of School.
354. Appointment of Board—Duties—Bond.
355. Industrial School Fund.
356. Fund to be Kept Separate.
357. Board May Receive Donations.

Section.
358. Donations, How Disposed of.
359. Work on Building, When Commenced.
360. Building, Cost of.
361. Grant of Site.
362. Deed of Site.

§ 353. (974.) Location of school.] The industrial school as established and located at the City of Ellendale in Dickey county, shall continue to be an industrial school and a school for manual training. Such school shall be governed by a board of trustees consisting of three members to be appointed as pre-scribed in the next section.

§ 354. (975.) Appointment of board. Duties. Bond.] At each biennial session of the legislative assembly, the Governor shall nominate, and, by and with the advice and consent of the senate, appoint a board of trustees for such school consisting of three members, who shall take charge and control of all funds in any manner accruing to the benefit or for the use of such school. Each member of such board shall qualify by taking and subscrib-ing the oath required of other civil officers and giving a bond in such sum and with such sureties as the Governor may require. They shall hold their office for the term of two years commencing on the first Tuesday of April succeeding their appointment and until their successors are appointed and qualified.

§ 355. (976.) Industrial school fund.] All funds arising from the sale, lease or use of the lands granted to such school, and the interest arising from the use or deposit of such funds, shall be kept and maintained for the purpose of creating an industrial school fund.

§ 356. (977.) Fund to be kept separate.] Such fund shall be kept as a separate fund by the State Treasurer, together with its increase, and shall be paid out only in the manner herein-after provided.

§ 357. (978.) Board may receive donations.] The board shall have power to receive all donations, gifts and bequests that may be offered or tendered to or for the benefit of such school, and shall on its order expend the money accumulated for the purposes herein provided for.

§ 358. (979.) Donations, how disposed of.] The board shall account to the Governor at least once in each year for all donations, gifts and bequests tendered and received, and all moneys coming into the hands of such board shall be immediately covered into the State treasury to the credit of the industrial school fund.

§ 359. (980.) Work on building, when commenced.] When-ever a sum not less than twenty-five thousand dollars shall have accumulated for the benefit of such school, the board may, after advertising for at least six weeks in a newspaper published at the seat of government and also in the county where such institution is located, let to the lowest responsible bidder a sufficient amount of work on the building herein contemplated to exhaust such sum, and may thereafter do likewise with any sum of not less than ten thousand dollars, until further provision shall have been made by the legislative assembly.

§ 360. (981.) Building, cost of.] Within two months after the appointment of the board herein provided for, it shall meet and determine the style, size and material of the building to be constructed, but in no case shall such building cost when com-pleted a sum exceeding one hundred and fifty thousand dollars.

§ 361. (982.) GRANT OF SITE.] This article shall become the law when a site for the school herein provided for shall have been granted absolutely to the State by the citizens of Ellendale, such site to contain not less than forty acres, and the selection and approval of the same shall be made by the board of trustees.

§ 362. (983.) DEED OF SITE.] When the site as herein provided for shall have been selected and approved, the deed for the same shall be filed in the office of the Secretary of State.

## ARTICLE XXXII.

### LIGNITE COAL TO BE USED.

Section.
363. -Public Institutions to Use.

§ 363. (1030.) PUBLIC INSTITUTIONS TO USE.] The various State institutions, county buildings and public schools of this State shall use for fuel native or lignite coal, and it shall be unlawful for any officer to purchase for use in such institutions, county buildings and public schools any coal other than that taken from the mines within the boundaries of this State. This section shall not be construed, however, as prohibiting the use of wood at such institutions, county buildings and public schools, when the cost thereof does not exceed that of native coal.

# PART III--SCHOOL AND PUBLIC LANDS.

## ARTICLE XXXIII.

### BOARD OF UNIVERSITY AND SCHOOL LANDS.

Section.
364. Board, How Constituted.
365. Board, Powers of.
366. Meetings of Board.
367. Board to Invest School Funds, How.
368. Records to be Kept by Secretary.
369. Treasurer Custodian of Funds.
370. Investments—How Unpaid Moneys to be Collected.
371. Manner of Investing Permanent Funds.
372. Incidental Expenses of Board, How Paid.
373. Appropriation for Interest.
374. Term of Office of Commissioner.
375. Salary of Commissioner.
376. Deputy Commissioner.
377. Duties of Commissioner.
378. County Board of Appraisal, Duties of.
379. Selecting and Certifying Lands for Sale.
380. Notice of Sale to be Published.
381. Manner of Sale.
382. Terms of Sale.
383. Adjournment of Sale.
384. Withdrawal of Lands from Sale.
385. County Auditor to Act as Clerk at Sale.
386. Notice to Purchaser—Execution of Contract.
387. Sales, When Void.
388. Surveys to be Made When Necessary.
389. Subdividing Land into Small Tracts or Lots, When to be Made.
390. Sale of Lots—New Appraisal.
391. Map to be Entered of Record.
392. Contracts of Purchase—Rights Under.
393. Assignee of Purchasers.
394. Contracts May be Surrendered and Two or More Issued, When.
395. Contract Void on Failure to Pay Principal, Interest or Taxes.
396. Redemption Before Re-Sale.
397. Fee in State until Contract Fulfilled.
398. Recovery of Possession.
399. Reconveyance to the United States.

Section.
400. Patents, When to Issue.
401. Patents to be Recorded.
402. Taxation of Lands After Sale—Purchaser of Tax Certificate.
403. Payment to County Treasurer—Duty of Treasurer.
404. Bond of County Treasurer—Conditions of.
405. Fees to County Treasurer.
406. Duty of County Auditor.
407. List of Lands Sold to be Furnished County Treasurer.
408. Township Assessors to Examine State Lands.
409. Transfer of Records to Commissioner.
410. Permanent and General Funds.
411. Quantity of Lands to be Sold.
412. Lands Subject to Lease.
413. Appraisal for Lease by County Board.
414. Selection of Lands for Lease.
415. Advertisement for Leasing.
416. Manner of Leasing—By Whom Made—How Conducted.
417. Deposit by Bidders—Forfeit on Failure to Pay.
418. Adjournment of Lease.
419. Approval of Lease and Execution of Contract.
420. Lessee not to Destroy Timber.
421. Lessee not to Break Uncultivated Land.
422. Hay not to be Cut Before July 10th.
423. Board May Grant Permits to Cut Hay, Remove Timber, Etc.
424. Trespass Upon Public Lands—Civil Action for.
425. Willful Trespass—Penalty.
426. Property to be Seized.
427. Damages.
428. State's Attorney to Prosecute and Report.
429. Expenses of Sale and Lease, How Paid.
430. Appropriation for Expenses of Board.

§ 364. (169.) BOARD, HOW CONSTITUTED.] The Governor, Secretary of State, State Auditor, Attorney General and Superintendent of Public Instruction shall constitute the board of university and school lands. The Governor shall be president; the Secretary of State, vice-president and the Superintendent of Public Instruction, secretary thereof. In the absence of the Superintendent of Public Instruction at any meeting of the board the Deputy Superintendent of Public Instruction shall act as secretary, but shall not be entitled to a vote. Such board, when acting as such, must act personally; no member can be represented on such board by any assistant or clerk.

§ 365. (170.)  BOARD, POWERS OF.]  Subject to the provisions of article 9 of the constitution and the provisions of this article, such board shall have the full control of the selecting, appraisement, rental, sale, disposal and management of all school and public lands of the State, including the real property donated to the Territory of Dakota under the provisions of chapter 104 of the laws of 1883, except such as has been sold, and the investment of permanent funds derived from the sale thereof, or from any other source, and shall have power to appoint a competent person to act as the general agent of the board in the performance of all its duties pertaining to the selection, sale, leasing or contracting in any manner allowed by law, and the general control and management of all matters relating to the care and disposition of the public lands of the State, all of whose official acts shall be subject to the approval and supervision of the board.  The title of such agent shall be Commissioner of University and School Lands, and before entering upon his duties as such he shall take the oath prescribed for civil officers and give a bond in the penal sum of ten thousand dollars, with not less than two sureties, to be approved by the board, and recorded in the office of the Secretary of State and filed, when recorded, in the office of the State Treasurer.

§ 366. (171.)  MEETINGS OF BOARD.]  Such board shall meet at the office of the commissioner on the last Thursday of each month, at ten o'clock in the forenoon.  Special meetings of the board may be held at any time at the written call of the president or any two members of the board.  Any three members of the board shall constitute a quorum.

§ 367. (172.)  BOARD TO INVEST SCHOOL FUNDS, HOW.]  Such board shall have the power and it is made its duty from time to time to invest any money belonging to any of the permanent funds of the common schools, university, school of mines, reform school, agricultural college and deaf and dumb asylum, normal schools, and all other permanent funds derived from the sale of public lands or from any other source, in bonds of school corporations within the State, bonds of the United States, bonds of the State of North Dakota, or in first mortgages on farm lands in the State, not exceeding in amount one-third of the actual value of any subdivision on which the same may be loaned, such value to be determined by the county board of appraisal of the respective counties, but such board shall not purchase or approve the purchase of any bonds or mortgages except at a legal session thereof, nor unless every member of the board is notified by the secretary of said board in time to be present at such meeting, and notified also that the question of purchasing or acting on a proposition for the purchase of certain bonds or mortgages is to be considered at the meeting, nor unless a majority of all the members vote in favor of such purchase, and the vote on the purchase of every bond and mortgage shall be taken by yeas and nays and shall be duly recorded in the books of the board.

§ 368. (173.) RECORDS TO BE KEPT BY SECRETARY.] The secretary shall enter in a suitable book kept for that purpose a full and correct record of all the proceedings of said board at each session thereof, which record when approved shall be signed by the president or presiding officer of the meeting and the secretary; he shall also keep such other books as may be necessary properly to register and describe all bonds and mortgages purchased or taken by it for the benefit of any of the permanent funds under its control. Such books shall be ruled so as to permit the registry of the name and residence of the person offering to sell any such bonds or mortgages, the district for which such offer is made, a description of the property covered by the mortgage, and a full and detailed description of every bond, whether United States, State or school district, and the date, number, series, amount and rate of interest of each bond, and when the interest and principal, respectively, are payable; and such record shall be made of every such bond and mortgage before the board shall act upon the question of purchasing the same. The secretary shall also keep in suitable books a record showing a detailed statement of the condition of all the permanent funds under control of said board, the amount of each fund, how invested, when due, interest paid and any other act in any manner connected with the management of said funds, and shall biennially report all such investments to the Governor, to be laid before the legislative assembly. All the records and record books of such board shall at all times be open for inspection by the public.

§ 369. (174.) TREASURER CUSTODIAN OF FUNDS.] All moneys belonging to the permanent funds of the common school and other public institutions derived from the sale of any of the public lands or from any other source shall be paid to and held by the State Treasurer, and be subject to the order of such board, and shall be paid over to the order of the board for investment as provided in section 172 of this article, whenever the board requires the same for such investment. The State Treasurer shall also be the custodian of all bonds, notes, mortgages and evidences of debt arising out of the management of the permanent funds derived from the sale of any of the public lands of the State or from any other source.

¹ § 370. (175.) INVESTMENTS. HOW UNPAID MONEYS TO BE COLLECTED.] It shall be the duty of the State Treasurer, from time to time as the same become due, to collect all moneys due and owing on any and all of the securities held by him for investment or for permanent funds, and from time to time, whenever required by the board, to make report of the amount of such collections to the board and a duplicate of the same to the State Auditor. If any such moneys shall remain unpaid for thirty days after the same shall become due and payable, he shall make report in detail of all such unpaid amounts to the Attorney

General, whose duty it shall be to proceed to collect the same by civil action, to be brought and prosecuted in the name of the State.

§ 371. (176.) MANNER OF INVESTING PERMANENT FUNDS.] In the investment of the permanent funds under its control such board shall authorize the State Auditor to draw his warrant on the State Treasurer, payable out of the proper fund, for the purchase of the bonds or mortgages, which warrant, previous to delivery, shall be registered by the State Treasurer in a book provided for that purpose.

§ 372. (177.) INCIDENTAL EXPENSES OF BOARD, HOW PAID.] The necessary incidental expenses of the board shall be paid out of the State Treasury, and upon satisfactory vouchers therefor the State Auditor shall issue his warrant for the same.

§ 373. (178.) APPROPRIATION FOR INTEREST.] There is hereby annually appropriated such sums as shall be found necessary for the expenses of purchase, and payment of accrued interest at the time of the purchase, of investment bonds or mortgages for the permanent funds under the control of said board, payable from the respective fund for which said purchase is made.

§ 374. (179.) TERM OF OFFICE OF COMMISSIONER.] The first term of office of the commissioner provided for in this article shall be for three years from the date of his appointment and until his successor is appointed and qualified, and after the expiration of the first term, all succeeding terms shall be two years, and until his successor is appointed and qualified, subject to removal by the board. In case of vacancy by death, removal, resignation or any other cause, the board shall fill the same by appointment.

§ 375. (180.) SALARY OF COMMISSIONER.] The commissioner shall receive an annual salary of two thousand dollars.

§ 376. (181.) DEPUTY COMMISSIONER.] By and with the consent of the board, the commissioner may appoint a chief clerk, who before entering upon any of the duties devolving upon him by said appointment shall take and subscribe the oath of office required by law and shall execute to the State a bond with one or more sureties in the penal sum of five thousand dollars conditioned for the faithful discharge of his duties.

§ 377. (182.) DUTIES OF COMMISSIONER.] The commissioner, under such directions as may be given by the board of university and school lands, shall have general charge and supervision of all lands belonging to the State, of all lands in which the State has an interest or which are held in trust by the State. He shall have the custody of all maps, books and papers relating to any of the public lands mentioned in this article. He shall procure the proper books, maps and plats in which to keep a complete record of all lands owned or held in trust by the State for schools, public buildings and for all other purposes, and shall keep true records of all the sales, leases, permits, patents, deeds and other conveyances of such lands made by the state, amount of money paid, date of sale and payment, description of land sold or leased, number of acres thereof, name of purchaser and designation of the fund that should be credited therewith. He shall direct all appraisements, sales, leases; shall execute all contracts of sale, leases, permits or other evidences of disposal of the lands, subject to approval by the board. Upon all contracts, leases or permits issued by the commissioner he shall certify the book and page where the same is recorded. He shall have an official seal with a proper device thereon; and the seal of the commissioner affixed to any contract of purchase, receipts or other instruments issued by him, duly countersigned by him as approved by the board, according to the provisions of this article, is *prima facie* evidence of the due execution of such contract or other paper. He shall biennially report to the legislative assembly through the board his work during the preceding term, showing the quantity of lands sold or leased, and the amount received therefor, the amount of interest moneys received to the credit of the several funds, expense of administration of his department, and all such other matters relating to his office as shall be necessary.

§ 378. (183.) COUNTY BOARD OF APPRAISAL, DUTIES OF.] The county superintendent of schools, the chairman of the board of county commissioners and the county auditor of each county shall constitute the "County Board of Appraisers" of the public lands of the state in and for their county. The county board of appraisal in each county shall upon the request of the board of university and school lands, designate on or before such date as it may specify, the public lands of the State in their county, that in its judgment can be sold for ten dollars an acre or upwards on the terms prescribed in this article, designating the tracts separately and giving an approximate estimate of their selling value. Thereupon the commissioner shall, if so ordered by the board of university and school lands, prepare a list and order an appraisal of such lands as shall be designated in such list, and it is made the duty of such board of appraisers within ten days after the receipt of such list to examine such lands and appraise them at their cash value, as nearly as can be determined, describing each tract or subdivision in parcels not greater than one hundred and sixty acres, more or less, according to the government survey, and in smaller subdivisions thereof if so listed by the commissioners, and set opposite each described tract or parcel of land the appraised value per acre thereof; and when such appraisal is completed, which shall not be later than thirty days after the receipt of the order directing it, the county board of appraisers, or the members of the same who made such appraisement, shall certify to its correctness, and make duplicate copies thereof, one of which shall be forwarded immediately to the board of university and school lands, and the other filed in

the office of the county auditor for reference. And in addition
to the appraisal òf such lands the county board of appraisal
shall furnish such other information regarding the lands as may
be required by the commissioner in the manner and form prescribed by him. The report of such appraisal shall be verified
by each of such appraisers and shall disclose any interest, real or
contingent, that any of such appraisers has in any of the lands
or improvements so appraised. Any appraiser who willfully
makes any false statement in such report, relative to such interest
in any of the lands so appraised, or improvements thereon, shall
be deemed guilty of a misdemeanor. For all services performed
under the requirements of this article the appraisers shall be paid
at the rate of three dollars per day and actual traveling expenses,
upon vouchers approved by the secretary of the board of
university and school lands to be paid by the State Treasurer
upon warrants issued by the State Auditor.

§ 379. (184.) SELECTING AND CERTIFYING LANDS FOR SALE.]
The commissioner shall from the list of lands so appraised and
reported by the county board of appraisers select all such tracts
as have been appraised at ten dollars per acre and upwards, and
upon approval of such selections by the board of university and
school lands shall make and certify to the county auditors the list
of lands in their respective counties that are offered for sale, and
when transmitting such list shall designate the day and hour for
the sale thereof; *provided*, that such sales shall take place only
between the hours of ten o'clock A. M. and five o'clock P. M. and
to be continued from day to day until all the lands advertised for
sale shall have been sold or offered for sale, except that adjourn-
ments may be made for any intervening Sunday or legal holiday.

§ 380. (185.) NOTICE OF SALE TO BE PUBLISHED.] The
county auditor shall immediately, on receipt of the list of lands
mentioned in the preceding section, cause to be published in a
paper designated by the county board of appraisers, as prescribed
by section 158 of the constitution, a notice of such sale, with the
list of lands properly described, that are to be offered for sale,
together with the appraised value thereof and the terms and
conditions of sale. The board of university and school lands
shall also publish notices of all sales for the same length of time
in one newspaper published at the seat of government.

§ 381. (186.) MANNER OF SALE.] On the day and hour
appointed for such sale the commissioner, except as hereinafter
provided, shall proceed to sell or offer for sale at public auction
to the highest bidder, at the court house or at the place where
the terms of the district court are held, of the county where the
lands are situated, the lands so advertised, offering them for sale
and selling in the order in which they occur in the advertisement
for sale. Such lands as have not been specially subdivided shall
be offered in tracts of one-quarter section, according to the subdivisions thereof by the United States survey, and those so

subdivided in the smallest divisions thereof. No tract shall be sold for less than its appraised value, and in no case for less than ten dollars an acre. Whenever the commissioner cannot attend the sale in person such sale may be made by the deputy land commissioner or any other person designated and authorized by the board of university and school lands.

§ 382. (187.) TERMS OF SALE.] Each tract of land shall be sold upon the following terms: The purchaser shall pay one-fifth of the price in cash at the time of sale, and the remaining four-fifths as follows: One-fifth in five years, one-fifth in ten years, one-fifth in fifteen years and one-fifth in twenty years, with interest at six per cent per annum on all the unpaid principal, annually in advance. The highest bidder for any offered tract shall be declared the purchaser thereof, and shall immediately pay over to the county treasurer the amount of one-fifth of the purchase price as specified in the terms of sale. In case the purchaser fails to pay the amount so required to be paid at the time of such sale, such commissioner or whoever may be conducting the sale, shall immediately re-offer such lands for sale, but no bids shall be received from the person so failing to pay as aforesaid; and the person refusing or neglecting to make such payment shall forfeit the sum of one hundred dollars for each tract so purchased by him.

§ 383. (188.) ADJOURNMENT OF SALE.] No adjournment of the sale can be made after its opening, except as provided in section 184 of this article, but, when the interest of the State will be subserved thereby, the board of university and school lands may, at any time not less than two weeks preceding the dates fixed for opening such sale, make an order postponing the same to such date as may be fixed in such order, which shall not be more than sixty days, giving due notice of the same to the county auditor, who shall publish such notice of adjournment and the day fixed for the same, for two successive weeks in the same papers in which the notice of sale is published; but the adjournment of any sale shall not require continued publication of the list of lands beyond the time specified in this article for such publication.

§ 384. (189.) WITHDRAWAL OF LANDS FROM SALE.] The board of university and school lands may, in its discretion, on or before the day of sale, withdraw any or all lands that may have been advertised for sale or included in any list to be offered in any county, and upon such withdrawal shall notify the auditor of such county, specifying the lands included in such notice of withdrawal, who shall thereupon strike such lands from the lists in his office, and public notice of withdrawal shall be given at the day of sale before any such lands are offered.

§ 385. (190.) COUNTY AUDITOR TO ACT AS CLERK AT SALE. APPROVAL OF SALE.] The county auditor shall act as clerk of all land sales and leases made in his county, and it shall be his

duty within five days after such sale or lease shall have been con-
cluded to certify to the board of university and school lands a
list of lands sold or leased as provided in this article, with the
price thereof and the name of the purchaser or lessee of such
tract, the amount for which the lands are sold or leased, the
amount of money paid by such purchaser, and the amount of
principal remaining unpaid, and the board of university and
school lands shall approve and confirm the sale or lease of every
such tract, as upon examination of such certified lists and such
further information and investigation as shall be deemed necessary, shall be found to have been sold or leased in accordance
with the law and without fraud or collusion. For the services
imposed by this article the county auditor shall be allowed the
sum of three dollars per day for each and every day so engaged,
to be paid out of any appropriation for the expenses of appraisal
and sale of public lands.

§ 386. (191.) Notice to purchaser. Execution of contract.] Immediately upon approval of the sales by the board
of university and school lands, the secretary of such board shall
prepare and certify a list of said approved sales to the commissioner, who shall without delay execute duplicate contracts in the
form prescribed by the board, and forward the same to the county
auditor of the county where the land was sold, whereupon it is
made the duty of the county auditor to notify each purchaser in
writing of the approval of the sale to him, and to appear within
ten days after the date of such notice and pay the county treasurer the amount of interest on the deferred payments as specified
in the contract and execute the contracts of sale, and a failure so
to appear and execute such contract shall act as a forfeiture of
the payment made by the purchaser ·at the sale. When the
contracts are properly executed by the purchaser and the amount
of money due thereon shall have been paid to the county treasurer the copy marked duplicate shall be delivered to him and the
original returned to the land commissioner, and each contract so
returned fully executed shall have on its face in the place noted
for such purpose the notation of the date of delivery to the, purchaser, and all contracts not executed by the purchaser shall be
returned to the land commissioner with a written statement
thereon of the reason for such return.

§ 387. (192.) Sales, when void.] Any sale made by mis-
take, or not in accordance with law, or obtained by fraud, shall
be void, and the contract of purchase issued thereon shall be of
no effect; but the holder of such contract shall be required to
surrender the same to the board of university and school lands,
who shall, except in case of fraud on the part of the purchaser,
cause the money to be refunded to the holder thereof.

§ 388. (193.) Surveys to be made when necessary.] Whenever it appears to the board of university and school lands necessary in order to ascertain the true boundaries of any tracts or

portions of lands, or to enable the commissioner to describe or dispose of the same in suitable and convenient lots, it may order all such necessary surveys to be made and,the expenses shall be paid out of the State treasury as other incidental expenses of the board of university and school lands are paid.

§ 389. (194.) SUBDIVIDING LAND INTO SMALL TRACTS OR LOTS, WHEN TO BE MADE.] Whenever in the opinion of the board of university and school lands the interests of the State will be promoted by laying off any portion of the land under its control into small parcels or city, town or village lots, the board may order such commissioner to cause the same to be done, and have the same appraised in the same manner as hereinbefore prescribed.

§ 390. (195.) SALE OF LOTS. NEW APPRAISAL.] All parcels or lots so appraised shall be subject to sale in the same manner and upon the same terms and conditions and the contract of purchase shall have the same effect, as in the case of other lands for which provision is made in this article, and at the prices at which the same are severally appraised, until a new appraisal is made, which the board of university and school lands may in its discretion order at any time, in the manner aforesaid, and with the like effect; but no lots or parcels so appraised shall be sold for less than the minimum price of said land, established in this article.

§ 391. (196.) MAP TO BE ENTERED OF RECORD.] Whenever the commissioner shall lay off any tract of land into small parcels or lots, as provided in this article, he shall cause a correct map of the same to be entered of record in the county where said lands are situated.

§ 392. (197.) CONTRACTS OF PURCHASE. RIGHTS UNDER.] Contracts of purchase, issued pursuant to the provisions of law, entitle the purchaser, his heirs or assigns, to the possession of the lands therein described, to maintain actions for injuries done to the same, or any action or proceeding to recover possession thereof, unless such contract has become void by forfeiture; and all contracts of purchase in force may be recorded in the same manner that deeds of conveyance are authorized to be recorded.

§ 393. (198.) ASSIGNEE OF PURCHASERS.] Each assignee of a *bona fide* purchaser of any of the lands mentioned in this article is subject to and governed by the provisions of law applicable to the purchaser of whom he is assignee; and he shall have the same rights in all respects as an original purchaser of the same class of lands.

§ 394. (199.) CONTRACTS MAY BE SURRENDERED AND TWO OR MORE ISSUED, WHEN.] Whenever the holder of any contract of purchase of any State or school land shall surrender the same to the commissioner with a request to have the same divided into two or more contracts, it shall be lawful for the commissioner to issue the same; *provided*, that the proposed subdivision shall be only in the smallest of the regular government or State subdivisions; and, *provided,* that no new contracts shall issue while there is due and unpaid any interest, principal or taxes on the principal contract of sale, nor in any case where the commissioner shall be of the opinion after an examination of the lands, if necessary, that the security would be impaired and endangered by the proposed division, nor until such proposed change shall have the approval of the board of university and school lands, and for all such new certificates a fee of five dollars for each certificate so issued shall be paid by the applicant, which fee shall be paid into the State treasury and become a part of the expense fund of the board of university and school lands.

§ 395. (200.) CONTRACT VOID ON FAILURE TO PAY PRINCIPAL, INTEREST OR TAXES.] In case the annual interest due on the first day of January in any year shall not be paid within ten days thereafter by the purchaser or by any person claiming under him, the contract shall, from the time of such failure, be void. In case any installment on the purchase price shall not be paid within ten days after the same becomes due by the provisions of contract of sale, the contract, from the time of such failure shall be void. And in case any of the taxes assessed against the lands described in any contract of sale for any year as provided for in this article shall remain unpaid on the second Monday of October of the following year, the contract shall be void. And in all cases where any contract becomes void by reason of failure to make the payments required by the contract and the terms of this section, it shall be the duty of the board of university and school lands to declare such contract of sale void, and notify the holder thereof of such declaration by written notice mailed to his post office address and to send a duplicate copy thereof to the auditor of the county in which such land is situated, and to order the commissioner to take possession of the land described in such contract.

§ 396. (201.) REDEMPTION BEFORE RE-SALE.] In all cases where the rights of a purchaser, his heirs or assigns, become forfeited under the provisions of this article, by failing to pay the amounts required, such purchaser, his heirs or assigns, may, before the re-sale at public auction of the lands described in such contract, pay to the State treasury the amount of interest due and payable on such contract, and all costs which have been incurred in addition thereto, together with interest at the rate of twelve per cent per annum on the interest and costs so due from the date of delinquency to the date of payment, and such payment shall operate as a redemption of the rights of such purchaser, his heirs or assigns, and such contract from the time of such payment shall be in full force and effect, as if no forfeiture had occurred; *provided,* that after the rights of a purchaser, his heirs or assigns shall have become forfeited under the provisions of this article, the board of university and school lands shall have the power, and it is hereby made their duty to provide for the re-sale of said land so forfeited if in their opinion a re-sale of said land shall be most advantageous to the State, otherwise the said board shall provide for the leasing of said land from year to year as herein provided, and after a lease of said land shall be made by said board, the lessee, his heirs and assigns, shall be entitled to the full and absolute possession of all of said lands and premises so leased.

§ 397. (202.) FEE IN STATE UNTIL CONTRACT FULFILLED.] The fee of each parcel of such lands shall be and remain in the state until the patents hereinafter provided for are issued for the same respectively, and no patent shall issue until full payment of all sums and full compliance with all the conditions of the contract of purchase, and in case of non-compliance by the purchaser, his heirs or assigns, with the terms of the contract as aforesaid, or with the provisions of law applicable thereto, any and all persons being or continuing in possession of any such lands after a failure to comply with the terms of the contract as aforesaid, or with such provisions of law, as aforesaid, without a written permission of the commissioner, shall be deemed and held to detain such land forcibly and without right, and to be trespassers thereon.

§ 398. (203.) RECOVERY OF POSSESSION.] In case any person holds or continues in possession of any of the land mentioned in this article, contrary to the conditions or covenants of any lease or written agreement, he shall be liable to an action of forcible detainer, or any other proper action for the recovery of possession of such lands and damages for detention of the same.

§ 399. (204.) RECONVEYANCE TO THE UNITED STATES.] In all cases where lands have been erroneously or improperly certified or conveyed to the State of North Dakota for school or other purposes by the United States, the Governor of the State is authorized to reconvey or relinquish by the execution, under his hand and the seal of the State, of such conveyances as will be necessary to convey or relinquish the title which the State may have to such lands.

§ 400. (205.) PATENTS, WHEN TO ISSUE.] When any land sold under the provisions of this article has been fully paid for, and all terms of the contract of purchase fully complied with, the board of university and school lands shall so certify to the Governor, who shall thereupon issue to the purchaser thereof, his heirs or assigns, a patent conveying the title of the State to such land, and the Governor shall in like manner issue a patent to any purchaser of the rights, title and interest of the original purchaser, his heirs or assigns, acquired by any execution sale. All such patents shall be signed by the Governor and attested by the Secretary of State with the great seal of the State of North Dakota, and shall be countersigned by the board of university and school lands with the seal of the secretary of said board.

§ 401. (206.) PATENTS TO BE RECORDED.] The registers of deeds of the several counties of this State are authorized to record all patents issued by the Governor pursuant to the provisions of this article; and the records thereof shall have the same effect as the record of other conveyances executed according to the laws of this State.

§ 402. (207.) TAXATION OF LANDS AFTER SALE. PURCHASER OF TAX CERTIFICATE.] The commissioner shall, as soon as possible after a sale of lands, transmit to the auditor of each county, in which any lands mentioned in this article have been sold, a detailed description of each parcel of the land so sold and the names of the purchasers, and the auditor shall extend the same upon his tax duplicate for the purpose of taxation, and the same shall thereupon become subject to taxation the same as other lands, and the taxes assessed thereon, collected and enforced in like manner as against other lands; *provided, however,* that the purchaser at tax sale of any such lands sold for delinquent taxes shall only acquire by virtue of such purchase such rights and interest as belong to the holder and owner of the contract of sale issued by such commissioner under the provisions of this article, and the right to be substituted in the place of such holder and owner of such contract of sale, as the assignee thereof; and upon the production to the proper officer of the tax certificate given · upon such tax sale, in case such lands have not been redeemed, such tax purchaser shall have the right to make any payment of principal or interest then in default upon such contract of sale, as the assignee thereof.

§ 403. (208.) PAYMENT TO COUNTY TREASURER. DUTY OF TREASURER.] The purchaser of any land mentioned in this article, or his assigns, may pay to the county treasurer of the county in which such land lies any amount which may be due from time to time on the contract, either for principal, interest, rents or penalty, and for the amounts so paid the county treasurer shall give to such person a duplicate receipt specifying the amount paid, date of payment, whether for principal, interest or penalty, and the fund to which it is applicable, the number of the contract, the name of the original purchaser of the land, or the assignee thereof, which receipt shall be countersigned by the auditor of said county, and have the same force and effect as if given by the State Treasurer. All moneys received by the county treasurer, under the provisions of this article, shall be held at all times subject to the order and direction of the State Treasurer for the benefit of the funds to which the moneys respectively belong; and during the months of January, March, June and October of each year, and such other times as he may be requested so to do by the State Treasurer, he shall pay into the State treasury all moneys received on account of such funds since the last payment he may have made.

§ 404. (209.) Bond of county treasurer. Conditions of.] The bond of each county treasurer shall be conditioned for the honest and faithful discharge of all trusts and responsibility imposed by this article, and for the faithful payment of and accounting for all moneys received by him under the provisions of this article to the State Treasurer or any other person entitled to receive the same, and the board of university and school lands shall on or before the first day of January, following any election for county officers, certify to the chairman of the board of county commissioners of each county the amount of money liable to come into the hands of the treasurer of the county under the provisions of this article, and the board of county commissioners shall add to the amount of the sum required on his regular official bond to the county double the sum so certified by the board of university and school lands, and the record of the proceedings of such board of county commissioners when fixing the amount of such bond shall specify in two separate items the aggregate amount of the bond so made up, designating one sum as the amount to indemnify the county, and the other to indemnify the State for any losses incurred by reason of failure to comply with the provisions of all laws regulating his duty.

§ 405. (210.) Fees to county treasurer.] County treasurers shall be entitled to a fee of one-half of one per cent on each dollar collected or received and remitted by them in payment of principal or interest, fines, penalties and damages on State lands, which fee shall be payable from the general fund of the class of lands on which payment is made to such treasurer, and such fee shall be paid to the county treasurer on vouchers countersigned by the county auditor and approved by the commissioner of university and school lands and such approved vouchers shall be paid out of any appropriation for the expenses of appraisement and sale of such lands.

§ 406. (211.) Duty of county auditor.] The county auditor shall, at the time he is required by law to return abstracts of settlement to the State Auditor, also forward all duplicate receipts of principal, interest or penalty on State lands, with a certified statement of such collections by the county treasurer, specifying the amount of each item; and he shall also make such return at any other time as may be required by the board of university and school lands.

§ 407. (212.) List of lands sold to be furnished county treasurer.] On or before the first day of December in each year the commissioner shall cause to be made out and transmitted to county treasurers a statement showing the lands sold in their respective counties, the number of the contracts of purchase, the name of the person to whom each contract was issued, and the amount of both principal and interest due on each on the first day of January, together with such directions, instructions and blanks as shall enable the county treasurers to carry out the provisions of this article.

§ 408. (213.) TOWNSHIP ASSESSORS TO EXAMINE STATE LANDS.] It shall be the duty of all township and district assessors, whenever required by the commissioner to examine and report on any lands designated to them by him, in the manner and form prescribed by him, and for such examination they shall be paid at the rate of three dollars per day for time actually engaged, upon vouchers approved by the commissioner.

§ 409. (214.) TRANSFER OF RECORDS TO COMMISSIONER.] All abstracts and conveyances of title to the State of North Dakota whether the said lands are held for penal, educational, charitable, school or other purposes, shall be, by those in whose charge such conveyances now are or may come, deposited with and remain in the control of the commissioner of university and school lands.

§ 410. (215.) PERMANENT AND GENERAL FUNDS.] The principal accruing from all sales of school, university or other State lands under the control of the board of university and school lands, as provided for in this article, shall become a part of the several permanent funds to which they respectively belong and shall not be reduced by any means whatever. All moneys received as interest, for rents, penalties, permits or from any source other than from the principal of sales shall become a part of the general or current funds to which they respectively belong and shall be distributed as directed by law.

§ 411. (216.) QUANTITY OF LANDS TO BE SOLD.] No more than one-fourth of the common school lands of the State shall be sold within the first five years after they become salable under the provisions of section 155 of the constitution, nor more than one-half of the remainder within ten years after the same become salable as aforesaid. The residue may be sold at any time after the expiration of such ten years; *provided, however*, that the coal lands of the State shall not be sold, but may be leased under the provisions of any law governing such leases. The words "coal lands" include lands bearing lignite coal.

§ 412. (217.) LANDS SUBJECT TO LEASE.] All the common school lands and all other public lands of the State that are not of such value as will admit of appraisal at ten dollars or more per acre, at the time of any regular appraisal, may be leased; *provided*, that no leases can be granted for a period longer than five years, and only for pasturage and meadow purposes, and at a public auction after notice as hereinafter provided; *provided, further*, that all of such school and public lands now under cultivation may be leased at the discretion and under the control of the board of university and school lands for other than pasturage and meadow purposes until sold. All rents shall be paid annually in advance.

§ 413. (218.) APPRAISAL FOR LEASE BY COUNTY BOARD.] It shall be the duty of the county board of appraisers, each and every year, if so ordered, to appraise in the same manner as all other lands that are listed for taxation are appraised all the common school and other public lands of the State in their respective districts that may be included in the order, making a return of all such appraisals to the board of university and school lands in the form prescribed on blanks furnished by the board; such returns to be made on or before the first day of July of the same year; and for any services performed as required by this article they shall be paid at the rate of three dollars per day, to be paid by the State Treasurer out of the funds appropriated for the current expenses of such board. It shall be the duty of the board of university and school lands to equalize the appraisements so returned as to counties by adding thereto or taking therefrom such a uniform percentage as may in its judgment seem proper and fair in order to arrive at a just and equitable equalization between the several counties, and upon such valuation so fixed the board of university and school lands are authorized to fix a per cent per acre as the minimum price at which the land can be leased; *provided*, that the lowest price of lands leased for pasturage cannot be below one-half of one per cent of the average value in the county, and for any cultivated lands in the county the lowest price cannot be below two and one-half per cent of the appraised value of each cultivated tract. And when advertising the same for lease they shall set opposite each description the value thereof as equalized by them, which valuation shall form the basis for leasing the same.

§ 414. (219.) SELECTION OF LANDS FOR LEASE.] The board of university and school lands shall have the power, and it is hereby made their duty to select from the lands so appraised such tracts as in the judgment of the board can be leased with profit to the school and other permanent land funds of the State, or as the legislative assembly may by law order to be leased, and shall on or before the first day of March in each succeeding year advertise for lease and offer for lease such lands as have thus been selected.

§ 415. (220.) ADVERTISEMENT FOR LEASING.] All such lands to be leased or offered for lease lying within the respective counties shall by the board of university and school lands be advertised for lease by publication once a week for not less than sixty days in some newspaper of general circulation in the vicinity of such lands. Such advertisement shall contain the designation or proper description of each tract or parcel of land so to be leased, the appraised value of each tract and the per cent on such valuation fixed by the board as the minimum price at which such land can be leased and the terms of the lease. A copy of such advertisement shall also be posted in a conspicuous place at the court house of the county, and a notice of the time and place where the said lands are to be leased shall also be published for not less than sixty days in one newspaper at the seat of government by such board of university and school lands; *provided*, that if in the opinion of the board there will not be sufficient of such lands situate in any county leased to pay the expenses of advertisement in a newspaper, the notice may be given by posting as aforesaid.

§ 416. (221.) MANNER OF LEASING. BY WHOM MADE. HOW CONDUCTED.] It shall be the duty of the commissioner of university and school lands, or such other person as may be appointed by the board of university and school lands, to conduct the leasing of such lands in accordance with the provisions of this article and such directions as shall be prescribed therefor by the board; *provided*, that the leasing shall be at public auction to the highest bidder at the court house or place where terms of the district court are held, commencing on the day specified in the advertisement for such lease and between the hours of ten o'clock A. M. and five o'clock P. M. to continue from day to day until all tracts or parcels of land advertised for lease shall have been leased or offered for lease; but the time for leasing the same shall not exceed ten days in any county, except that an adjournment may be made over the Sabbath or any legal holiday. In counties where a large number of tracts of land are to be leased the land situated in certain townships may be designated in the advertisement to be leased on certain specified days and in such case such lands shall be leased or offered for lease on such specified days, or for want of time for the leasing or offering for lease of all such designated lands, the leasing of those unoffered may be adjourned until the following day or days, when they must be the first lands offered for lease. Such lands as shall not have been specially subdivided shall be leased or offered for lease in tracts of one-quarter section each, and those so subdivided in the smallest subdivision thereof. Notice must be given when the land is offered that all bids are subject to approval by the board. At the time of offering the lands for lease the county auditor of the county shall act as clerk, and it shall be his duty to make report thereof, stating the terms of such leasing, as is prescribed in section 190 for making reports of sales.

§ 417. (222.) DEPOSIT BY BIDDERS. FORFEIT ON FAILURE TO PAY.] In offering any tract or parcel of land no bid shall be entertained until the bidder therefor shall deposit fifty per cent of the minimum price fixed in the advertisement, which deposit, should he be the successful bidder, shall be applied as part payment on the lands so leased by him, but should he fail to pay the balance required on his bid he shall forfeit the money so deposited. Deposits by all unsuccessful bidders shall be returned to them. All competitive bids shall be on the basis of so many dollars premium over and above the minimum price at which the tract is offered. The annual rent in all cases of lease shall be payable in advance as hereinafter provided.

§ 418. (223.) ADJOURNMENT OF LEASE.] Whenever the board

of university and school lands finds that the interests of the State will be subserved by the adjournment of the time for offering lands for lease, the authority conferred by section 188 for adjournment of sales is made applicable to the leasing of lands.

§ 419. (224.) APPROVAL OF LEASE AND EXECUTION OF CONTRACT.] Immediately upon the receipt of the report of the county auditor as required by this article the board of university and school lands shall approve and confirm the lease of all such tracts as in their judgment should be made, and shall at once certify a list of the approved leases to the commissioner who shall without delay execute duplicate contracts of lease in the form prescribed by the board and forward the same to the county auditor of the respective counties where the land was leased, who shall notify each lessee in writing to appear within ten days after date of notification and pay the county treasurer the amount of money required to complete the contract, and execute such contract of lease; and a failure to appear and execute the contract shall forfeit the deposit made at time of the bid. When the contract is properly executed by the lessee and the amount of money due thereon shall have been paid to the county treasurer, the copy marked " duplicate " shall be delivered to him and the original thereof shall be returned to the commissioner, and each contract fully executed and so returned, shall have on its face in the place noted for such purpose the notation of the date of delivery to the lessee, and all contracts not executed by the lessee shall be returned to the commissioner with a written statement thereon of the reason that they are not executed.

§ 420. (225.) LESSEE NOT TO DESTROY TIMBER.] No lessee of any of the common school or public lands of the State, or his heirs or assigns, shall cut down or take away from such tract any timber, trees or wood, or suffer or cause the same to be done by any person, except that such lessee may cut down or use such amount of dead, or prostrate trees, or timber as may be sufficient to supply him with fuel for his family or the families of his employees actually residing upon such tract. Any lessee violating the provisions of this section shall forfeit his lease and all rights and interests thereunder, and shall be liable to the State for damages sustained by the State by reason thereof, and shall be guilty of a misdemeanor.

§ 421. (226.) LESSEE NOT TO BREAK UNCULTIVATED LAND.] No lessee, or the heirs or assigns of any lessee, of any of the common school or public lands of this State, leased for meadow or pasturage purposes, or of school or public lands leased for the purpose of cultivation, which may contain any uncultivated or unbroken land, shall break, plow or cultivate any unbroken land on any tract so leased, or cause or suffer it to be done by any other person. And any lessee, or his heirs or assigns, who shall violate the provisions of this section shall incur the same forfeitures and liabilities as are provided in the preceding section, and shall also be guilty of a misdemeanor.

§ 422. (227.) HAY NOT TO BE CUT BEFORE JULY 10TH.] No lessee, or his heirs or assigns, shall mow or cut for hay or feed any grass on any unbroken land, or cause or suffer the same to be done by any other person prior to the tenth day of July in any year. And any lessee, or his heirs or assigns, who shall violate the provisions of this section shall incur the same forfeitures and liabilities as are provided in section 225 and shall also be guilty of a misdemeanor.

§ 423. (228.) BOARD MAY GRANT PERMITS TO CUT HAY, REMOVE TIMBER, ETC.] The board shall have authority, when in its judgment it is for the best interests of the State so to do, to sell the right to cut grass on any of the public lands of the State and to sell any fallen and dead timber on such lands for such price and on such terms and conditions as it may think proper; *provided,* that all such permits shall be only for the current season and between the fifteenth day of June and the first day of April of the following year, and that the control or rights of occupancy of such lands shall be only such as is specified in such permit, and the board of university and school lands may appoint as local agents to carry out the provisions of this section the chairman of the board of township supervisors in organized townships, the commissioner of any district where the townships are not organized, or any other suitable person who is a resident of the township where the public lands are situated, who upon accepting such appointment and before entering upon his duties as such agent shall take and subscribe an oath or affirmation justly and impartially to perform the duties of his office to the best of his ability, which oath shall be recorded in the office of the Secretary of State and filed in the office of the board of university and school lands. The duties of such agent shall be prescribed by the commissioner, to be approved by the board of university and school lands, and compensation for his service shall be fixed by the board, based upon a percentage of the amounts of money collected and remitted to the State Treasurer from the sale of grass and timber in his township or district.

§ 424. (229.) TRESPASS UPON PUBLIC LANDS. CIVIL ACTION FOR.] Whoever commits any trespass upon any of the lands owned, or held in trust, or otherwise by the State shall be liable in treble damages in an action to be brought in the name of the State, if such trespass is adjudged to have been willful; but single damages only shall be recovered in such action if such trespass is adjudged to have been casual and involuntary.

§ 425. (230.) WILLFUL TRESPASS. PENALTY.] Whoever commits any willful trespass upon any of the lands owned or held in trust or otherwise by this State, either by cutting down or destroying any timber or wood standing or growing thereon, or by carrying away any timber or wood therefrom, or by mowing or cutting or removing any hay or grass standing or growing or being thereon, or who injures or removes any buildings, fences, improvements or other property belonging or appertaining to said land or unlawfully breaks or cultivates any of said lands or aids, directs or countenances such trespass or other injury shall be deemed guilty of a misdemeanor, and on conviction thereof shall be punished by imprisonment in the county jail not more than one year, or by fine not exceeding five hundred dollars, or both such fine and imprisonment, in the discretion of the court. And whoever is occupying, residing upon or in possession of any school or other public lands owned or held in trust or otherwise by the State at the time of the passage, approval and taking effect of this act without a valid lease therefor shall be deemed and held to be a willful trespasser thereon, and guilty of trespass upon such land, and upon conviction thereof shall be punished as provided for in this section for any other act of trespass.

§ 426. (231.) PROPERTY TO BE SEIZED.] In addition to the penalties provided for in this article against those committing trespass upon any of the lands owned or held in trust or otherwise by this State, the commissioner is authorized and empowered without legal process to seize and take, or cause to be seized and taken any and all timber, grass, wood or other property unlawfully severed from such lands, whether the same has been removed from such lands or not, and may dispose of the property so seized and taken, either at public or private sale, in such manner as will be most conducive to the interests of the State; and all moneys arising therefrom after deducting the reasonable and necessary expenses of such seizure and sale shall be made a part of the general fund belonging to the public lands and shall be distributed in accordance with the provisions of this article.

§ 427. (232.) DAMAGES.] All damages recovered for any trespass, or other injury upon or to any of the lands mentioned in this article, shall be paid over to the State Treasurer for the benefit of the general fund to which the same properly belongs.

§ 428. (233.) STATE'S ATTORNEY TO PROSECUTE AND REPORT.] The State's Attorneys of the several counties shall promptly report to the commissioner all cases of trespass committed upon such lands, which may come to their knowledge, and shall, when directed by the Attorney General, prosecute all actions for any trespass or injury thereto, or for recovery of possession thereof, or otherwise.

§ 429. (234.) EXPENSES OF SALE AND LEASE, HOW PAID.] The expenses of publishing notices of the leasing and sale of the university, school and all other public lands of the State shall be paid by the State Treasurer upon the warrant of the State Auditor out of the general or current funds of the different institutions as designated in section 215, and such expenses shall be apportioned according to the receipts credited each fund from proceeds of each and every sale or lease. All bills for such publishing shall be verified by the publisher and approved by the board of university and school lands.

§ 430. (235.) APPROPRIATION FOR EXPENSES OF BOARD.] There is hereby annually appropriated out of any funds in the treasury not otherwise appropriated the sum of five thousand dollars, or so much thereof as may be found necessary, for the salaries and expenses of the commissioner of university and school lands, clerk hire, record books, blanks and all such other expenses as shall be necessarily incurred by the board of university and school lands in carrying out the provisions of this article, and such expenses shall be paid out of the treasury, and upon satisfactory vouchers therefor the State Auditor shall issue his warrant for the same.

# APPENDICES.

## APPENDIX A.

### SPECIAL LAWS.

The following special laws enacted by the legislative assembly from 1877 to June 20, 1886, pertaining to the organization and government of independent school districts and acts amendatory thereof are in full force and effect, to-wit:

(*a*) "An act providing a board of education for the City of Fargo, Dakota Territory, and regulating the management of the public schools therein," approved February 20, 1879.

(*b*) "An act providing for a board of education for the City of Jamestown, Dakota Territory, and regulating the management of the public schools therein," approved March 3, 1883.

(*c*) "An act establishing school district No. 3 (Grafton) of Walsh County, Dakota Territory, as an independent school district," approved March 9, 1885.

(*d*) "An act providing for a school board for the City of Lisbon, and for other purposes," approved March 13, 1885.

(*e*) "An act incorporating the City of Mayville, Traill County, Dakota Territory," approved March 13, 1885.

(*f*) "An act to create certain territory now within the school township of Brightwood, Richland County, Dakota Territory, as an independent school district, No 1 (Hankinson,) Richland County, Dakota Territory," approved March 13, 1885.

(*g*) "An act establishing the independent school district of Walcott, Richland County, Dakota Territory," approved March 13, 1885.

(*h*) "An act to create a joint school township (Waziya) in the counties of Griggs and Steele," approved March 13, 1885.

All other special and private laws pertaining to the establishment and management of schools in that portion of the Territory of Dakota which now constitutes the State of North Dakota, have expired by their own limitation, or otherwise.

# APPENDIX B.

LAWS PERTAINING TO SPECULATION IN OFFICE AND PENALTY FOR
FAILURE TO MAKE REPORTS—BLANKS TO BE FURNISHED.

### SPECULATION IN OFFICE PROHIBITED.

§ 7632. (PENAL CODE.) UNLAWFUL PURCHASES BY SCHOOL
DISTRICT OFFICERS.] Every person who while an officer of any
school district or corporation, or deputy or clerk of such officer,
directly or indirectly, buys or traffics in or in anywise becomes a
party to the purchase of any school warrant, order or scrip, or
any bill, account, claim or evidence of indebtedness against his
school district or corporation, for any sum less than the full face
value thereof, is guilty of a misdemeanor, and upon conviction
thereof is punishable by a fine of not less than fifty and not
exceeding five hundred dollars.

### PENALTY FOR FAILURE TO MAKE REPORTS.

§ 306. (POLITICAL CODE.) PENALTY.] Any county, city,
village, civil township, school township or school district officer,
who is required by law to make an official report to any other
county, city, village, civil township, school township or school
district officer, board, tribunal or state officer, and who willfully
neglects to make such report, or fails to perform such official
duties, shall forfeit and pay to the State a penalty of not less than
ten nor more than two hundred dollars, to be recovered from
such delinquent officer, or from him and the sureties upon his
official bond, in a civil action to be brought by the State's
Attorney in any court of record having jurisdiction.

§ 307. EXAMINATION OF RECORDS. STATE'S ATTORNEY TO
PROSECUTE.] It shall be the duty of the board of county commissioners and the State's Attorney in each county to examine
the records of the several county officers at the end of the
officer's term of office to see that they have been properly kept.
Any failure must be remedied or it shall become the duty of the
State's Attorney to prosecute any such officer for neglect as provided in the last section. It shall also be the duty of the city
council, board of aldermen, village trustees, civil township supervisors, school township or school district board, as the case may
be, to examine the records of their several officers in a like
manner, or upon complaint by the proper board the State's
Attorney shall prosecute as provided in the last section.

§ 308. BLANKS TO BE FURNISHED.] It shall be the duty of
the county, city, village, civil township, school township or school
district officers to provide at the expense of the county, city,
village, civil township, school township or school district, such

blanks and records as are necessary for making the proper record and the transaction of any official business connected with his office.

## APPENDIX C.

### FILING BOND OF TREASURER.

§ 346. (POLITICAL CODE.) BONDS OF TOWNSHIP AND SCHOOL DISTRICT OFFICERS.] It shall be the duty of each county auditor on or before the first day of March in each year to procure the proper blank bonds and send them to the clerk of each township and school district, and all such officers required by law to give bonds shall procure such bonds from the proper clerk; and shall immediately after the execution and approval thereof hand the same to the clerk of the township, whose duty it shall be forthwith to file such bonds, except those of justices of the peace, with the county auditor, and the county auditor shall on receipt thereof examine such bonds and see that they are properly executed and, if he finds that any bonds are not executed according to law, he shall note thereon any errors and return them to the clerk for correction, and it is hereby made the duty of the clerk to have such bonds corrected forthwith and return the same to the county auditor. The county auditor shall not issue any order upon the county treasurer for funds or money belonging to a civil township or school district to any person as treasurer of such township or school district until his bond has been filed as in this section provided.

## APPENDIX D.

### BONDS FOR LABOR AND MATERIAL FOR PUBLIC BUILDINGS.

§ 4802. (CIVIL CODE.) BONDS FROM CONTRACTORS ON PUBLIC IMPROVEMENTS.] Whenever any public officer shall, under the laws of this State, enter into contract in any sum exceeding one hundred dollars, with any person for making any public improvements, or for constructing any public building, or making repairs on the same, such officer shall take from the party contracted with a bond, conditioned to the effect that such contractor shall pay all indebtedness incurred for labor or material furnished in the construction or repair of such public building or in making such public improvements.

§ 4803. HOW BOND EXECUTED.] Such bond shall run to the State of North Dakota, shall be executed by two or more sureties and shall be for an amount at least equal to the price stated in the contract. It shall be approved by the clerk of the district court of the county in which said building is to be constructed or such public improvement is to be made and the sureties thereon shall qualify in a sum equal to double the amount specified in the bond.

§ 4804. WHERE BOND FILED. RECOVERY ON.] Such bond shall be filed in the office of the clerk of the district court of the county in which such public improvement is to be made or such public building is to be erected; and any person to whom there is due any sum for labor or material furnished, as stated in section 4802, or his assigns, may bring an action on the bond for the recovery of such indebtedness; *provided*, that no action shall be brought on such bond unless commenced within one year from the completion of such public improvements, repairs or buildings.

## APPENDIX E.

### DIGEST OF DECISIONS OF SUPREME COURT.

#### SCHOOL DISTRICTS—POWERS.

Laws Dak. 1879, Chap. 14, Sec. 29, Subd. 4, provides that the inhabitants qualified to vote at a school district meeting may vote for a site for a school house. By Subdivision 5, they may vote a tax to purchase or lease such site. By Section 56, it is made the duty of the district board "to purchase or lease such site for a school house as shall have been designated by the voters at a district meeting," and to build such a school house as the voters of the district shall have agreed upon. *Held*, that the power to acquire a site for a school house is vested exclusively in the voters of the district, and the board have no independent authority whatever.

*Farmers' and Merchants' Nat. Bank of Valley City vs. School Dist. No. 53, Barnes County, 42 N. W., 767.*

The statute restricts the amount of obligations a school district may incur in any one year to 1½ per cent on the value of the taxable property in the district. *Held*, that warrants payable immediately, for sums exceeding such percentage, are invalid. *Id.*

The district may plead *ultra vires* to an action on warrants issued for the purchase of a school site by the district board without authority. *Id.*

#### SCHOOLS AND SCHOOL DISTRICTS—TAXATION—CONTRACTS.

Laws Dak. 1879, Chap. 14, Sec. 29, Subd. 5, provides that school district may vote annually a tax of 1 per cent on the taxable property of the districts to purchase or lease a site for a school house. Subdivision 8 provides that school districts may vote a tax as may be necessary, not exceeding one-half per cent in any one year, to furnish the school with furniture and apparatus. A school board issued orders in excess of 1½ per cent of the taxable property in the district, on which they obtained money, which was used in purchasing a site and building, and furnishing a school house; and, on completing the school house two years thereafter, reported such orders, showing that they amounted to less than 1½ per cent tax for each of the two years would have produced, and the district accepted and occupied the school house, and approved the report. *Held*, that' the district had power to issue the orders, and had ratified the action of the board in issuing them, and was bound thereby.

*Capital Bank of St. Paul vs. School Dist. No. 85, Cass County 42 N. W., 774.*

SCHOOLS AND SCHOOL DISTRICTS—INCORPORATION—BONDS—ESTOPPEL.

Pol. Code Dak. 1877, Chap. 40, Sec. 10, provides that "it shall be the duty of the county superintendent of schools * * * to divide his county into school districts, subdivide and rearrange the boundaries of the same, when petitioned by a majority of the citizens residing in the district or districts to be affected by said change and to furnish the county commissioners * * * with a written description of the boundaries of each district, which description must be filed in the register of deeds' office before such district shall be entitled to proceed with its organization." *Held*, that a petition by a majority of the citizens of the districts affected is a condition precedent to the incorporation by the superintendent of a new district.

*Dartmouth Sav. Bank vs. School Dists. Nos. 6 and 31, Minnehaha County, 43 N. W., 822.*

In an action on a bond issued by a district formed without such petition against districts which are its successors, defendants are not estopped to deny that district's incorporation by showing failure to present the petition. *Id.*

SCHOOL DISTRICTS—TEACHER'S SALARY—WARRANTS.

Every contract relating to the employment of a teacher who does not hold a lawful certificate of qualification is void by the express terms of the statute, and every warrant issued in payment of services of such teacher is without consideration and void.

*Goose River Bank vs. Willow Lake School Tp., Steele County, 44 N. W., 1002.*

School township warrants are not negotiable instruments, in the sense that their negotiation will cut off defenses to them existing against them in the hands of the payee. *Id.*

The officers of a school township cannot estop the township by a representation, express or implied, that the facts to authorize the issue of a lawful warrant exist. *Id.*

Where a contract is expressly prohibited or declared void by statute, retention of the fruits of such contract will not subject a municipality to liability under the contract or on a *quantum meruit*. *Id.*

A person who assists a public officer in depriving the public of the benefits of a statutory protection designed to guard the people against unfit and incompetent teachers has no standing in court, and his assignee will receive no greater consideration. *Id.*

*Coler et al. vs. Dwight School Tp., of Richland County.*
[Supreme Court of North Dakota.  April 25, 1893.]

SCHOOL TOWNSHIP—ESTOPPEL—EXISTENCE OF DISTRICT.

1.  The county superintendent of schools, under Chapter 14, Laws 1879, organized a school district.  School district officers were elected, and exercised the functions of their respective offices; teachers were employed by the district, and school was taught therein, and a school meeting was held in the district to vote upon the question of issuing bonds to build a school house. Such bonds were thereafter issued.  In an action upon some of the interest coupons of such bonds, *Held,* that the district was a *defacto* municipal corporation, and that therefore the defense could not be interposed that the bonds were void on the ground that the district had no legal existence because of a failure to comply with provisions of the statute regulating the organization of such districts in matters which went to the jurisdiction of the county superintendent to organize the district.

2.  Municipal corporations are estopped, as against *bona fide* holders of municipal bonds, from setting up as a defense to an action thereon that all the preliminary steps necessary to authorize the issue of the bonds were not taken, when the officers who have charge of the issue of such bonds are especially or impliedly authorized to determine whether all the conditions precedent to the issue of valid bonds have been complied with, and recite in the bonds so issued that they have been complied with. It is not necessary to estop the corporation that this statement should set forth in detail that all the preliminary steps have been taken.  It is sufficient that it declare that the bonds are issued in pursuance of a certain statute, specifying it.  Neither is it essential that the officers issuing the bonds should be expressly authorized to determine such questions.  It is sufficient if they are given full control in the matter.

3.  A school township organized under Chapter 44, Laws of 1883, becomes, immediately upon such organization, liable for debts of a district, the school house and furniture of which become the property of the school township.  This liability is complete, and does not depend upon the settlement of equities between several districts included in the new school township, under Sections 136–138, c. 44, Laws 1883.

[*Syllabus by the Court.*]

*Prairie School Township vs. Haseleu et al.*
[Supreme Court of North Dakota, July 6, 1893.]

SCHOOL DISTRICTS—POWERS OF OFFICERS—LOSS OF FUNDS—LIA-
BILITY OF TREASURER ON OFFICIAL BOND—PAROL EVIDENCE—
HARMLESS ERROR.

1. Chapters 44-45, Sess. Laws Dak. T. 1883, relating to school townships and school house bonds, considered. *Held*, that the school board (consisting of the treasurer, clerk and director) is the official governing board of such school township, and such board has full power and authority to issue, negotiate and sell such bonds of the school township as have been duly voted by the electors for the purpose of building a school house. *Held, further*, that the school township treasurer, acting independently, has no authority under the law and by virtue of his office as treasurer, to issue, negotiate or sell such bonds.

2. Where the school board of the plaintiff, consisting of the treasurer, clerk and director, issued certain school house bonds, which had been regularly voted by the electors, and in doing so delivered such bonds to a bank to be negotiated and sold for the benefit of the school township, and the bonds were sold and put in circulation, but the proceeds were never turned over to the school township, but, on the contrary, were lost to the school township, *Held*, that the school board was wholly responsible for such loss. *Held, further*, that such bonds not having been delivered to the treasurer for negotiation and sale, and he never having sold or attempted to sell the same, an action will not lie against the treasurer or his sureties on his official bond for a breach of the condition of such bond, which requires the treasurer to account for and pay over all moneys and property which shall come into his hands as treasurer.

3. The obligations of sureties upon official bonds are measured by the language of the bond, and where the condition of a bond embodies the provision of the statute, and no more, the obligation cannot be expanded by construction beyond the fair import of the language in which the sureties have consented to be bound.

4. When the bonds were delivered by the board at the bank for negotiation and sale, all members of the board were at the bank, and acting in concert. At that time the cashier of the bank delivered to the treasurer a writing as follows: "$1,000. Grand Rapids, Dakota, Sept. 28th, 1883. Received of William Haseleu, Treas. Prairie School Township, one thousand dollars in bonds of Prairie Tp., LaMoure Co., D. T., for placing and cr. A. H. Huelster, Cashier Bank of Grand Rapids." *Held*, that such writing embodied both a receipt and a contract, and that, as such its terms could be varied and explained by parol evidence, but only as to that part which is a mere receipt.

5. Where it appears that upon the uncontroverted facts the plaintiff cannot recover in the action, a verdict and judgment for defendants will not be disturbed by this court even when the records show errors in procedure. Such errors are without prejudice.

[*Syllabus by the Court.*]

*Gull River Lumber Company, Plaintiff and Respondent, vs. School District No. 39, Barnes County, D. T., Defendant and Appellant.*

### I. PRACTICE—FINDINGS OF FACT.

When the trial court determines the issue of fact without a jury, the requirement of the statute as to findings is mandatory, and not directory. In such cases it is the duty of the trial court without request to make express findings of the ultimate facts which are material and arise upon the pleadings. Accordingly when the district court, in such case, made no express findings of the ultimate facts which were in issue, but instead of doing so adopted certain documentary evidence, and a certain stipulation of facts, as its findings of facts, and from such findings drew certain legal conclusions, upon which judgment was entered, *Held*, reversible error.

### 2. CAPITAL BANK VS. SCHOOL DISTRICT FOLLOWED.

Merits of this case same as decided at present term of court, *i. e.*: *Capital Bank of St. Paul vs. School District No. 53.*

*Gull River Lumber Company vs. School District No. 39, of Barnes County.*

### I. TRANSFER OF CAUSES UNDER THE OMNIBUS BILL.

Respondent, after the admission of North Dakota into the Federal Union, argued the appeal in this case in the Supreme Court of the State, applied for a rehearing after defeat, and after securing a rehearing applied for and obtained a continuance. *Held*, that he could not thereafter obtain a transfer of the case to the Federal Court on the ground of diverse citizenship, under the provisions of the enabling act.

[Opinion filed Feb. 2, 1891.]

*Capital Bank of St. Paul, Plaintiff, Appellant vs. School District No. 53, Barnes County, D. T., Defendant and Respondent.*

### I. SCHOOL DISTRICT—CONTRACT ULTRA VIRES—RATIFICATION.

A contract, authorized by the inhabitants of a school district at a district meeting, to build a school house for an amount in excess of funds on hand or subject to collection for that purpose, and the amount that could be realized from the maximum tax which could be levied by the inhabitants for the current year and used for that purpose, is void. Therefore, *Held*, that such a contract, void because the district board had no authority to make it, could not be made binding upon the district by subsequent ratification by the inhabitants. Whether there were sufficient evidence of such ratification not decided.

2. SAME—RECEIPT OF FRUITS OF CONTRACT CREATES NO LIABILITY.

Such contract being impliedly prohibited by statute, the receipt by the district of the fruits thereof creates no liability either under the contract or for the value received.

3. SAME—WARRANT CREATES NO LIABILITY.

A warrant creates no greater liability than the debt it represents, whether in the hands of the original party or of a purchaser before maturity and for value.

[Opinion Filed Nov. 29, 1890.]

*Goose River Bank vs. Gilmore, et al.*
[Supreme Court of North Dakota, Jan. 25, 1893.]

APPEAL FROM ORDER DENYING NEW TRIAL—RECORD.

1. When an appeal is taken from an order denying a new trial, and the motion for new trial was heard in part upon certain papers and documents, which, on appeal to this court, have been properly identified by the Judge and certified by the clerk of District Court, a motion to purge the record of such papers and documents for the reason that the same are not authenticated by any bill or statement, cannot be sustained. Under Section 5, c. 120, Laws 1891, no bill or statement is required to bring such papers and documents before the court.

2. The stenographer's transcript of the proceedings had at the trial, and used on a motion for a new trial for the purpose of showing errors of law occurring at the trial, does not constitute an authenticated record and before this court can review errors occurring at the trial, the proceedings must be brought upon the record by a bill of exceptions or statement of the case.

3. An affidavit used upon a motion for a new trial, which states that certain evidence could and would be offered if a new trial should be granted, is entirely insufficient unless it also states that such evidence is newly discovered, or furnishes some excuse for not introducing it on the former trial.

[*Syllabus by the Court.*]

# APPENDIX F.

## JANUARY.

1st—School year begins. Section 128.

First Monday (odd numbered years)—Terms of office of State Superintendent and county superintendent begin. Sections 1 and 17.

Second Tuesday—Regular meeting of district school board. Section 60.

Second Tuesday—District treasurer makes report. Section 96.

Third Tuesday—District school board makes settlement with district treasurer. Section 96.

Second Friday—County examination for teachers. Section 119.

Between 1st and 31st—District clerk and clerk of board of education furnish report to county superintendent. Sections 86 and 176.

## FEBRUARY.

Third Monday—Apportionment of State Tuition Fund. Section 90.

## MARCH.

Second Friday—County examination for teachers. Section 119.

## APRIL.

Second Tuesday—Regular meeting of district school board. Section 60.

## MAY.

Second Friday—County examination for teachers. Section 119.

Third Monday—Apportionment of State Tuition Fund. Section 90.

## JUNE.

At least fifteen days before third Tuesday—District school board designates polling place and causes three notices of election to be posted. Section 53.

Third Tuesday—Annual school election at 2 p. m. Sections 49 and 53.

Within five days after annual election—Clerk to furnish each person elected a written notice of election. Section 56.

Within ten days after annual election—District clerk forwards to county superintendent a certified list of all officers elected. Section 56.

## JULY.

1st.—Assessor furnishes school district clerk, county superintendent and auditor the amount of assessed valuation. Section 103.

Second Tuesday—Regular meeting of district school board. Sections 60 and 172.

Second Tuesday—District school board organizes and elects a president and clerk. Section 59.

Second Tuesday (on or before)—School treasurer gives bond and qualifies. Section 63.

Second Friday—County examination for teachers. Section 119.

Before 20th—District school board and board of education levy tax. Sections 78 and 100.

Immediately thereafter—District clerk and clerk of board of education notify county auditor the amount levied. Sections 100 and 180.

## AUGUST.

15th (on or before)—County superintendent transmits annual report to State Superintendent.

Third Monday—Apportionment of State Tuition Fund. Section 90.

## SEPTEMBER.

Second Friday—County examination for teachers. Section 119.

## OCTOBER.

Second Tuesday—Regular meeting of district school board. Section 60.

## NOVEMBER.

1st—(On or before, in even numbered years)—State Superintendent makes report to the Governor. Section 14.

First Tuesday after first Monday (in even numbered years) -Election of State Superintendent and county superintendent. Sections 1 and 17.

Second Friday—County examination for teachers. Section 119.

Third Monday—Apportionment of State Tuition Fund. Section 90.

## DECEMBER.

1st—District clerk makes enumeration of school children in the district. Section 86.

Before 20th—District clerk and clerk of board of education forward to county superintendent enumeration of school children. Sections 86 and 95.

31st (On or before in even numbered years)—The report of the State Superintendent is printed. Section 15.

31st—School year ends. Section 128.

# INDEX.

## ACADEMY OF SCIENCE AT WAHPETON
object of .................................................................... 105
management of.............................................................. 105
rules and regulations of.................................................. 105, 106
how located ................................................................ 20
board, how appointed ...................................................... 105
powers of board.... ....................................................... 105
expenses of board—temporary funds, how secured........................ 106
land grant, etc............................................................ 106
state treasurer custodian of funds......................................... 107
record of board ........................................................... 107

## ACCOUNTS
to be itemized before audited and paid ................................... 19
of district treasurer, how to be kept .................................... 49
(uniform system of keeping—See Political Code, Sects. 309-321.)

## ACTION
to be commenced against district treasurer, when......................... 39

## ADJUSTERS
of whom composed.......................................................... 52
to assess taxes in certain instances...................................... 52

## ADVERTISEMENT
of lands to be leased..................................................... 133
of lands to be sold ...................................................... 124

## AGRICULTURAL COLLEGE AT FARGO
course of study in, what length of....................................... 108, 109
honorary degrees, conferred upon whom.................................... 110
lands granted for ........................................................ 11
how located .............................................................. 19, 107
treasurer................................................................. 110
meetings—compensation.................................................... 108
acceptance of land grant................................................. 110
duties of board.......................................................... 108
salaries of faculty...................................................... 109
rules and regulations ................................................... 109
president's duties—reports............................................... 109
experiment station ...................................................... 110
per diem and mileage of board........................................... 108

## ANNUAL
meeting of board of education in special districts....................... 72
election ............................................................... 34, 35, 71

## APPARATUS
to be furnished by district board ....................................... 40

S. L.—II.

## APPEALS

may be taken from county superintendent's decision.... ............ 27
from county superintendents to be decided by state superintendent..... 24

## APPENDICES

........................................................................ 139

## APPORTIONMENT

of state tuition fund, to be made by county superintendent............ 28, 48
of state tuition fund, how made..................................... 48

## APPRAISAL OF SCHOOL LANDS

for sale........................................................... 123, 127

## APPRAISERS

of school lands.................................................... 123

## APPROPRIATION

for institute, by county commissioners ............................. 62

## ARBITRATION

equalization of indebtedness of joint district, how arrived at......... 54
tax to pay joint debts to be levied................................ 54
result to be sent to county auditor............................... 54

## ASSESSMENT

to meet interest and provide sinking fund ......................... 68

## ASSESSOR

to notify district clerk valuation of property ...................... 52
to report number of deaf and dumb children....................... 112

## ATTORNEY GENERAL

member of board of university and school lands.................... 16, 119
to give opinions to board of university and school lands............ 144
to cause trespassers upon school lands to be prosecuted............ 144
duty to prosecute officers who fail to make report ................. 148

## BIBLE

may be read in school ............................................ 61
not sectarian book................................................ 61

## BLANKS

to be furnished by state department............................... 23

## BLIND ASYLUM

location............................................................ 20, 114
trustees, how appointed........................................... 115
organization of board ............................................ 115
meetings—compensation........................................... 115
land grant—proceeds ............................................. 20, 116
rules of regulation................................................ 116
reports........................................................... 116

## BOARD OF APPRAISAL

of school lands, of whom composed............................... 16, 123

## BOARD OF EDUCATION

in independent districts, how elected............................. 82
in cities incorporated under special law .......................... 89
method of disorganizing independent districts and equalizing debts.... 89, 90

## BOARD OF UNIVERSITY AND SCHOOL LANDS

of whom composed........................................................... 16, 110
authority—meeting of—secretary ......................................... 120
ex-officio recorder.......................................................... 121
investment of school funds................................................ 120, 121
records..................................................................... 121
state treasurer custodian of funds......................................... 121
governor to issue patents................................................... 120
when lands subject to taxation ............................................. 130
patents, how recorded...................................................... 130
expenses of sale and lease, how paid....................................... 137
appropriation for expenses of board........................................ 138

## BOND

required of treasurer of special district................................... 75
required of district treasurer, how approved............................... 38
additional, when required of district treasurer............................. 38
of district officer, where to be filed....................................... 39, 141
of district treasurer to be filed before apportionment is paid to him ..... 48
of treasurer of independent school district................................. 85
of treasurer of agricultural college........................................ 110

## BONDS

school district bonds, how issued........................................... 66
notice of election to vote................................................... 67
denomination of bonds—rate of interest—limit of issue.................... 67
record of bonds to be kept by clerk......................................... 67, 68
assessment for sinking fund and to meet interest.......................... 68, 84
bonds, how negotiated—not to be sold below par........................... 69
county auditor may levy tax to pay bonds.................................. 69
security for payment of bonds.............................................. 79
cancelled bonds, record of to be made by clerk............................ 69
proposals for building school house ....................................... 69
bonds may be voted and issued to meet indebtedness already incurred
    for building school houses............................................. 70
of special district, how may be issued .................................... 78
investment of sinking fund................................................. 68, 79
authority to issue in independent school districts.......................... 84
power of board in special school districts to refund....................... 80
for labor and material, for public buildings............................... 141

## BOUNDARIES

of school district.......................................................... 30
of school district, how may be changed.................................... 31
in district counties, how to be rearranged................................. 32
how changed in future..................................................... 33

## BRANCHES OF STUDY

required for county certificates............................................ 57
required for professional and normal certificates ......................... 55, 56
what to be taught in common schools...................................... 60
additional, may be fixed by board ......................................... 41

## CALENDAR

............................................................................ 148

## CANCELLED BONDS

record of, to be made by clerks............................................ 69

## CENSUS

(See Enumeration.)

CERTIFICATES
  (See Examinations and Certificates.)
  professional .................................................. 55
  normal........................................................ 56
  county ....................................................... 56, 57
  how revoked .................................................. 56, 58
  permits, when allowable....................................... 57
  when should be revoked ....................................... 28

CHARTS
  to be furnished by district board ............................ 40

CHAIRMAN OF BOARD OF COUNTY COMMISSIONERS
  member of board of appraisal of school lands ................. 16

CHILD LABOR
  prohibited during school hours................................ 64

CITIES
  what, governed by provisions of article relating to special districts....... 70

CIVIL TOWNSHIP
  to be the boundaries of what school districts................. 30

CLERK OF DISTRICT
  to keep record of bonds ...................................... 68
  to keep record of cancelled bonds............................. 69
  penalty for neglect of duty, and for making false election returns....... 2
  penalty for false reports..................................... 66
  to be clerk of election ...................................... 36
  to issue certificates of election to district officers ....... 36
  how appointed................................................. 37
  duties of and compensation ................................... 37
  to notify county auditor of tax levy ......................... 42
  to enumerate school children in the district................. 45
  to make annual report, when................................... 45
  to give notice of tax levy to county auditor ................. 51
  vacancy of, how filled ....................................... 53
  teacher's report to be filed with ........................... 59

CLERK OF SPECIAL DISTRICT
  duties of..................................................... 73
  to give certificates of election to members of board......... 77

COMMON SCHOOLS
  sections 16 and 36 granted for support of.................... 9
  lands granted for use of, may be sold, when.................. 16
  length of terms required to be taught........................ 43, 44
  additional time may be taught................................ 44

COMPULSORY ATTENDANCE
  school age, time required to attend school................... 63
  who exempt from attending school ............................ 63
  penalty for failure to send children to school.............. 63
  duty of president of board to prosecute...................... 64
  president subject to fine if he does not prosecute........... 64
  child labor prohibited during school hours................... 64
  penalty for employing children during school hours.......... 64
  prosecution, how brought .................................... 64

CONSOLIDATION
  of districts, when required.................................. 32

## CONDUCTORS OF INSTITUTES
how appointed ............................................................... 24, 62
certify expenses to state superintendent of public instruction ............ 61

## CONTRACTS
made with teacher, who does not hold certificate, void .................. 58
terminated when certificate revoked ..................................... 58
for more than certain sums to be advertised ............................. 66, 75
members of board of education not to be interested in ................... 72
with teachers to be in writing .......................................... 41
for lease of school lands, how executed ................................. 134, 135
of sale of school lands, how executed ................................... 126
of sale of land void when taxes not paid ............................... 128

## CONVEYANCE
of property to special districts, how executed .......................... 71

## CONSTITUTIONAL PROVISIONS
### THE LEGISLATIVE DEPARTMENT
local or special laws not to be passed by legislative assembly ........... 13

### EXECUTIVE DEPARTMENT
superintendent of public instruction, how chosen ....................... 13
qualifications for ...................................................... 13
office where to be held ................................................. 13
powers and duties of ................................................... 13
salary of ............................................................... 13

### ELECTIVE FRANCHISE
electors, qualifications of .............................................. 14
privileged from arrest at election ...................................... 14
when does not lose his residence ........................................ 14
soldiers, seamen and marines in the army and navy not electors ......... 14
persons under guardianship, non compos mentis, or insane not entitled
    to vote ............................................................. 14
women may vote for all school officers and on school matters .......... 14
elections to be by secret ballot ........................................ 14

### EDUCATION
why necessary ........................................................... 14
provision to be made for public schools ................................. 15
public schools to be open to all children of the state .................. 15
to be free from sectarian control ....................................... 15
uniform system to be provided for ...................................... 15
truthfulness, temperance, etc., to be taught in ........................ 15
county superintendent of schools to be elected ......................... 15
illiteracy to be prevented .............................................. 15
colleges, universities and institutions receiving aid from or supported
    by the state, to be under its control .............................. 15
sectarian school not to receive money raised for support of common
    schools ............................................................ 15

### SCHOOL AND PUBLIC LANDS
per centum from sale of, gifts and other property acquired, the state to
    make permanent fund ............................................... 15
principal of such fund, to remain inviolate ............................ 15
state to make good losses thereof ...................................... 15
interest and income of permanent fund, to be apportioned between the
    several common schools of the state ............................... 15, 16
portion apportioned and not expended to become part of school fund ... 16
lands granted to state may be sold after one year from assembling of
    first legislative assembly ......................................... 16

SCHOOL AND PUBLIC LANDS—Continued.

lands, when and how may be sold.................................................... 16
coal lands of the state not to be sold.............................................. 16
board of university and school lands, who compose............................ 16
authority of board of university and school lands............................. 16
appraisal of school lands to be made by county superintendent of
    schools, chairman of the county board and county auditor............. 16
minimum price and terms at which land may be sold...................... 16
lands, how to be advertised for sale ............................................ 17
grant or patent for lands, when to issue........................................ 17
lands, subject to taxation, when.................................................. 17
lands, and proceeds from sale of, etc., to be applied to specific purpose
    for which granted .................................................................. 17
lands granted to several institutions, how to be appraised and sold...... 17
when may be sold..................................................................... 17
leasing of lands, how to be provided for........................................ 17
lands, for what purposes, may be leased........................................ 17
moneys of permanent school fund, how to be invested..................... 18
claims for improvement on school lands not to be recognized............. 18
state school funds to be guarded by suitable laws............................ 18
by bonds of officers charged with keeping the same........................ 18
conversion of moneys belonging to state fund to be felony................ 18

PUBLIC DEBT AND PUBLIC WORKS

limit of indebtedness by any political subdivision ........................... 18
indebtedness of political subdivision, how to be estimated................. 18
evidence of indebtedness in excess of legal limit allowed, to be void.... 19
tax to meet indebtedness to be provided before it is incurred.............. 19
political subdivisions prohibited from making certain loans, etc......... 19
bills against political subdivisions to be itemized before audited and
    paid.................................................................................... 19
evidences of indebtedness to have indorsed certificate of proper officer,
    that the same is legal, and within the debt limit........................... 19

PUBLIC INSTITUTIONS

permanently located .................................................................. 19
where and what located.............................................................. 19, 20
grants of lands to..................................................................... 19, 20
similar ones, not to be located except by revision of the constitution.... 20

COUNTY AUDITOR

member of the board of appraisal of school lands............................ 16
to prepare a plat of county......................................................... 34
to levy poll tax and 2 mill tax for school purposes.......................... 51

COUNTY COMMISSIONERS

to organize new district, when.................................................... 30
may appropriate money for institutes ........................................... 62
to pay transportation of indigent deaf and dumb children to school.... 113
duties of in relation to joint school districts.................................. 31
to rearrange and establish boundaries of school districts .................. 32

COUNTY SUPERINTENDENT OF SCHOOLS

election—term of office.............................................................. 15, 26
in case of tie vote, how to proceed.............................................. 36
general duties of ..................................................................... 26
record of official acts ............................................................... 27
to furnish assessors with sectional maps....................................... 27
meetings with school officers ..................................................... 27
to decide questions of controversy .............................................. 27
power to administer oaths........................................................... 27
power to revoke certificates........................................................ 28

## COUNTY SUPERINTENDENT OF SCHOOLS—Continued.

institute fund—how raised, how used ............................................. 27
apportionment of state tuition fund ............................................. 28
teacher's certificates—when revokable ......................................... 28, 58
report to state superintendent ................................................... 28
duties in relation to appraisement of school lands—fees ................... 28
office rent, postage and stationery ............................................. 28
salary—deputy—traveling expenses, etc ....................................... 28
qualifications of ................................................................. 29
to give notice of election ....................................................... 35
duty in relation to bonds of school district officers ....................... 39
duty in relation to county institutes .......................................... 61, 62
to apportion school funds ....................................................... 48
vacancy—how filled .............................................................. 53
to hold public examination of teachers ....................................... 56
member of county board of appraisal .......................................... 16, 123
duties in relation to lease of school lands ................................... 132
duties in relation to sale of school lands .................................... 123
to take and subscribe to oath of office (see Sec. 341, Political Code)
to require new bond of district treasurer, when ............................. 38
duty to prosecute district treasurer on bonds, when ........................ 39
to apportion state tuition fund ................................................ 48
to certify to county treasurer and county auditor amount of tuition fund
   due each district ............................................................. 48
to notify district treasurer of amount of tuition fund due each district .. 48
to report institute fund on hand to state superintendent annually ....... 61

## COUNTY TREASURER

to return to state treasurer unpaid state tuition fund ..................... 46, 47
pay over funds to district treasurer, when ................................... 49
to keep account with school corporations ..................................... 50
to collect school taxes ......................................................... 50
fees to .......................................................................... 131

## COURSE OF STUDY

to be prescribed by state superintendent ..................................... 24

## DAMAGES

for trespass upon school lands, how collected ................................ 136
collected for trespass, to be paid to state treasurer ....................... 137

## DEAF AND DUMB ASYLUM

who may receive an education in ................................................ 111
county assessors to report names, etc., of deaf and dumb persons for .... 112
account for clothing of pupils, how collected ................................ 112
transportation of indigent persons to, how paid ............................. 113
how located ...................................................................... 20, 111
management ....................................................................... 111
organization of board—meetings ................................................ 111
duties of board .................................................................. 111
indebtedness limited—per diem and mileage ................................... 112
fee for non-resident pupils ..................................................... 112
faculty—duties of principal—salary ............................................ 113
matron ........................................................................... 114
report of board .................................................................. 114
compulsory education of certain children ..................................... 63

## DEBT

for school house may be paid by bonds, how .................................. 70
limit of .......................................................................... 18

## DECISIONS
county superintendent to decide all school matters of controversy
arising in county .......................................................... 27
appeal from, how taken.................................................... 27

## DECISIONS OF SUPREME COURT
school districts, power to vote tax....................................... 142
taxation, contracts........................................................ 142
bonds, estoppel............................................................ 143
teachers not having certificate cannot collect wages...................... 143
school district treasurer, school warrants, when not valid................ 143

## DEPUTY
county superintendent may appoint..................................... 28, 29

## DICTIONARY
Webster's unabridged, to be furnished by district board.................... 40

## DIRECTORS
election of ............................................................... 34
vacancy in office of, how filled .......................................... 53
penalty for neglect of duty of............................................. 65
terms of office of......................................................... 34
to take and subscribe to oath of office ................................... 37
to constitute district school board........................................ 37
necessary for a quorum .................................................... 37
meetings of—fees .......................................................... 37
one to be chosen president of board........................................ 37
salary of.................................................................. 37
to approve district treasurer's bond—to require new bond, when........... 38

## DISSOLVE
special district may—how.................................................. 76

## DISTRIBUTION
of supplies by county superintendent...................................... 26

## DISTRICTS
(See School District and Special Districts.)

## DISTRICT CLERK
(See Clerk of District.)

## DISTRICT LIBRARIES
information to be furnished by state superintendent of public instruction .................................................................. 23, 24
district school board may purchase ........................................ 40

## DISTRICT SCHOOL BOARD
general powers—power to establish schools................................. 40
repairs, fuel, supplies, furniture, maps, register, district library, dictionary, etc., to be furnished by........................................... 40
teachers, how employed—certificate required by teacher—contract to be
in writing ............................................................ 41
admission of pupils from other districts, when............................. 41
rules—suspension of pupils................................................ 41
branches of study......................................................... 41
tax levy to be notified to county auditor................................. 42
school houses may be used for other purposes than school, when and
how .................................................................. 42
school houses and sites, how to be determined ............................ 42
election for selection of site and erection of school house............... 42
real property for school house sites how obtained......................... 43

## DISTRICT SCHOOL BOARD—Continued.

schools to be organized on petition................................................ 43
school terms, how arranged—when school may be discontinued.......... 43
additional school time, when.................................................. 44
district high schools, how established............. .......................... 44
school census—clerk's annual school report, when made.................... 45
clerk's report to be examined by board....................................... 45
records open to inspection ..................................................... 45
only|English language to be taught............................................ 45
vacancy in office of director or treasurer—how filled....................... 53
vacancy in office of clerk—how filled ........................................ 53
penalty for neglect of duty ................................................... 65
use of school funds for private use an embezzlement........................ 65

## DISTRICT SCHOOL OFFICERS

board of directors............................................................. 37
organization of—clerk........................................................ 37
meetings of board—fees of members........................................... 37
duties of president........................................................... 37
duties of clerk—compensation................................................. 37
treasurer's bond, how approved—vacancy, how filled......................... 38
additional bond of treasurer, when required................................. 38
school funds, how paid out.................................................... 38
warrants to be indorsed, when funds not in treasury to pay................. 38
warrants—what to specify ..................................................... 39
oaths and bonds, where to be filed........................................... 39
salary of school treasurer.................................................... 39
prohibited from speculating in office........................................ 140
penalty for failure to make reports.......................................... 140
vacancies in office, how filled............................................... 53
not to be interested in contracts, or speculate in school securities ........ 65
must deliver public property to successors, (see Sec. 358, Political Code.)

## DISTRICT TREASURER

election of.................................................................... 34
vacancy in office of, how filled ............................................. 53
penalty for neglect of duty of ............................................... 65
not to use school funds for private purposes................................. 65
penalty for failure to pay over funds and to make proper indorsement
on unpaid warrants ...................................................... 65, 66
penalty for false reports..................................................... 66
to take and subscribe to oath of office ...................................... 37
to give bond—bond, how approved............................................. 38
failure to give additional bond—vacates office............................... 38
to keep accounts, make reports and pay money only on warrants........ 38
to indorse warrants when there are no funds to pay......................... 38
to keep separate account of state tuition fund............................... 46, 47
accounts of, how to be kept................................................... 48, 49
to make reports in triplicate................................................. 49
annual report in triplicate................................................... 49

## DISTURBANCE

of public schools............................................................. 66

## DUTIES

(See Powers, Rights and Duties.)

## DUTIES OF TEACHERS

notice of opening and closing school.......................................... 50
when teacher not entitled to compensation .................................... 59

## DUTIES OF TEACHERS—Continued.

teacher's register, what to contain ............................................. 59
school year and school week defined—holidays.......................... 59
branches to be taught in public schools.................................... 60
teachers required to attend institute—penalty for failure to attend...... 60
pupils may be suspended for cause........................................ 60
assignment of studies to pupils........................................... 60
Bible not sectarian book, may be read by teacher...................... 61
teacher to give moral instruction to pupils.............................. 61

## EDUCATION

why necessary................................................................ 14

## ELECTION

date of for district school directors............... .................... 34
for school, treasurer............................................ ..... 34
terms of office of school officers...................................... 34
first election in any district to be arranged for by county superintendent 35
qualifications of school electors and school officers.................... 35
of county superintendent................................................. 35
hours polls open—notices of annual election.......................... 35
judges of election........................................................ 36
votes, how canvassed.................................................... 36
certificates of election................................................. 36
oath of school officers.................................................. 37
of boards of education in special districts............................. 72
to vote bonds ............................................................ 67
notice of election of board............................................. 81
election precincts—canvass of returns................................ 81
certificates of election.................................................. 82
to vote bonds in special districts ...................................... 78
notice of to vote bonds.................................................. 67
penalty for false returns of ............................................ 65
to be by secret ballot.................................................... 14
of boards of education in special districts............................. 76
of state superintendent................................................. 13, 23
in case of a tie vote, how to proceed .................................. 36
notice of, for board in independent districts.......................... 81
of board of education in cities working under special charter........ 89

## ELECTION PRECINCTS

in special districts....................................................... 77

## ELECTORS

qualifications of ......................................................... 14
privileged from arrest, when............................................ 14
when do not lose residence ............................................. 14
certain persons who are not............................................. 14
who entitled to vote...................................................... 14, 35

## EMBEZZLEMENT

treasurer guilty of, when................................................ 65

## ENABLING ACT, PROVISIONS OF

public schools to be provided for...................................... 9
public schools, to be open to all children............................. 9
public schools, to be free from sectarian control..................... 9
sections 16 and 36 granted for support of common schools........... 9
indemnity lands granted, in lieu of school sections taken............ 9
mineral lands............................................................. 11
lands in Indian, military and other reservations, not granted......... 9
lands granted for educational purposes not to be sold for less than $10 per
acre.................................................................. 9, 10

## ENABLING ACT, PROVISIONS OF—Continued.

lands reserved for school purposes may be leased under certain conditions ... 9, 10
per centum of proceeds of public lands granted to school fund ............ 10
university, lands granted for ............................................. 10
schools, colleges and universities, to be under control of state ............ 10
sectarian schools, not to receive any proceeds of sale of lands ............ 10
agricultural college, lands granted for ................................... 10, 11
school of mines, lands granted ........................................... 11
reform school, lands granted for ......................................... 11
normal school, lands granted for .......................................... 11
capitol building, lands granted for ........................................ 11
educational and charitable purposes, lands granted for ..................... 11
lands to be held, appropriated and disposed of as legislature provides... 11
mineral lands, exempted from grant ....................................... 11
lands granted, how to be selected ......................................... 11

## ENDORSEMENT

to be made on warrants when not paid...................................... 38

## ENGLISH LANGUAGE

records to be kept in..................................................... 45
only, to be taught in public schools ....................................... 45

## ENUMERATION

of children of school age in special districts............................... 74
of children in district, by clerk, when to be made.......................... 45
copy of, to be filed in clerk's office and another sent county superintendent............................................................. 45

## EQUALIZATION

of debts and property in special district................................... 76

## EXAMINATIONS AND CERTIFICATES

question for examination of applicants for teachers' certificates........... 55
professional certificates, who entitled to.................................. 55
normal certificates, who entitled to....................................... 56
fee for issuing a certificate—certificate, how revoked...................... 56
examination of teachers by county superintendent.......................... 56
teachers' grades, how established ......................................... 57
re-examination of papers by state superintendent, when allowed......... 57
qualification of teachers ................................................. 57
fee for certificate—certificate when revokable............................. 58
in proceedings to revoke certificate, teacher given opportunity to make defense ............................................................. 58
examination for county certificates, when held............................. 56
questions and rules for, prescribed by state superintendent............... 24

## EXPENSES

of state superintendent................................................... 25
of county institutes, how paid ........................................... 61, 62

## EXPERIMENT STATION

(See Agricultural College.)

## FEE

for examination for state certificate ...................................... 56
for examination for county certificate .................................... 58
for re-examination by state superintendent................................ 57
from examination, to be turned over to county treasurer for institute fund ................................................................ 27

## FEES

(See Salary and Fees.)

## FINES, FORFEITURES AND PENALTIES

penalty for neglect of duty of school director, treasurer or clerk..........  65
penalty for false election returns....................................................  65
school officers not to be interested in contracts or speculate in school
    securities................................................................................  65
use of school funds for private use an embezzlement.......................  65
penalty for failure of treasurer to pay over ...................................  65, 66
penalty for failure to make proper indorsement on warrant as required
    of treasurer ...........................................................................  66
penalty for false report by clerk or treasurer...................................  66
penalty for willful disturbance of public schools .............................  66
proposals for contract, violation of a misdemeanor..........................  66
penalty for violating compulsory attendance law .............................  63, 64
fines collected under article relating to compulsory attendance to be
    paid into school fund................................................................  64

## FLAGS

purchase of by school board................................................................  91

## FORM

of notice of annual school district election......................................  35
of oath, judges and clerks of election to take.....................................  36
of oath, directors and treasurer to take..............................................  37
of clerk's notice of tax levy..............................................................  51

## FORESTRY, SCHOOL OF

where located.....................................................................................  20

## FORFEITURES

(See Fines, Forfeitures and Penalties.)

## FREE TEXT BOOKS

school board authorized to purchase, when......................................  90
proposition submitted to voters at annual election...........................  90
petition for vote to adopt.....................................................................  90

## FUEL

to be supplied by district board .......................................................  40

## FURNITURE

of school house, to be furnished by district board .............................  40

## GOVERNOR

member of the board of university and school lands........................  16, 119
to issue patents, when.......................................................................  129
ex-officio member board of directors for normal schools...................  101

## GRADUATES

of state university entitled to certificates, when.........................55, 56, 97, 98

## HAY

on rented school lands not to be cut before July 10............................  136

## HEALTH AND DECENCY IN PUBLIC SCHOOLS

duty of district boards and boards of education..............................  93

## HIGH SCHOOL

to be maintained by special district .................................................  73
how may be established in school districts........................................  44
how much school session required in..................................................  44

## HIGH SCHOOL BOARD

of whom composed .............................................................................  91
classification of high schools.............................................................  91
requirements for classification..........................................................  92

## HIGH SCHOOL BOARD—Continued.
high schools to be visited............................................. 92
members serve without compensation............................... 92
discretionary powers of board....................................... 92
records to be kept..................................................... 92

## HOLIDAYS
school not to be taught on............................................ 59

## INDEPENDENT SCHOOL DISTRICTS
organization on petition—notice of election........................ 81
ballots—returns....................................................... 81
board of education, how elected..................................... 82
date of election—canvass, etc........................................ 82
vacancies, how filled................................................. 82
powers of board of education—meetings............................ 82, 83
secretary and duties.................................................. 83
levy of tax—amount of tax limited.................................. 83, 84
bonds, authority to issue............................................. 84
moneys, how paid out—bond of treasurer........................... 85
school funds, how kept................................................ 85
general powers of board.............................................. 85
non-resident pupils................................................... 87
title to school houses and sites..................................... 87
real property how conveyed........................................... 87
report of city treasurer.............................................. 87
city council to pass certain ordinances............................. 88
forfeit for failure to serve on board when elected................. 88
new district to assume debts of old district........................ 88
method of disorganizing.............................................. 89

## INDUSTRIAL SCHOOL
how located.......................................................... 20, 116
appointment of board—duties—bond.................................. 117
fund—donations....................................................... 117
building—cost of..................................................... 117
grant of site—deed................................................... 118

## INSTITUTE
how noticed.......................................................... 60
penalty for failure to attend........................................ 60
county institute fund, how created.............................. 27, 61, 62
state institute fund.................................................. 62
institute conductors................................................. 62
state institute fund, how paid out.................................. 62
appropriation for, by county commissioners........................ 62
rules for, to be prescribed by state superintendent................ 24
conductors to be appointed by state superintendent............... 24, 62
state superintendent to assist at.................................... 25

## INSTITUTE FUND
how raised........................................................... 27

## INTEREST
rate of, on bonds.................................................... 67
rate of, on warrants................................................. 38, 39

## JUDGES OF ELECTION
appointment of....................................................... 35

## JUDGMENT
levy of tax to pay................................................... 51, 52

## LEASE
of school lands, how executed........................................ 135

## LEASING OF LANDS
how to be provided for............................................. 17
for what purpose lands may be leased.............................. 17
advertised........................................................ 133
how leased........................................................ 134
how conducted..................................................... 134
adjournment of.................................................... 134
approval of....................................................... 135

## LIBRARY
appropriation for state educational library....................... 91
for university.................................................... 99

## LIGNITE COAL
public institutions to use........................................ 118

## LIMIT
of issue of bonds................................................. 67
of indebtedness................................................... 18
of tax levy that may be made...................................... 42

## LOAN
of muskets to university.......................................... 99

## MAPS
to be furnished by district board................................. 40
to be furnished to assessors by county superintendent of schools.. 27

## MAXIMUM TAX LEVY
for final judgment................................................ 51, 52
to pay equalized indebtedness..................................... 52
for all school purposes........................................... 50

## MEETINGS
county superintendent to arrange for, with school officers........ 27
of board of education in special districts........................ 72
of district school board.......................................... 37
of state superintendent with county superintendents............... 24

## MILEAGE
of county superintendent.......................................... 29

## MORAL INSTRUCTION
to be given all pupils............................................ 61

## NAME
of school district................................................ 32
of special district............................................... 71

## NEGOTIATION
of bonds, how may be made......................................... 69

## NEW DISTRICTS
how formed........................................................ 31

## NORMAL CERTIFICATES
.................................................................. 56

## NORMAL SCHOOL BOARDS
state superintendent of public instruction ex-officio member of... 23

## NORMAL SCHOOLS

location ................................................................................... 19, 20, 101
endowment ................................................................................ 101
land grant ........................................................................... 11, 19, 20
government and management ...................................................... 101
board of trustees ..................................................................... 101
meetings of board—officers ....................................................... 102
compensation .......................................................................... 102
funds, how kept ...................................................................... 102
accounts, how audited and paid ................................................ 102
course of study ...................................................................... 102
direction of expenditures ................................................... 102, 103
powers and duties of board of management .............................. 103
report .................................................................................... 103
employment of faculty ............................................................. 103
faculty, duties of .................................................................... 103
duty of principal ..................................................................... 103
reports .................................................................................. 104
diplomas—state certificates, etc ............................................... 104

## NOTICE

of election to vote bonds ......................................................... 67
of election in special districts ................................................... 78
of annual district election ....................................................... 35
of tax levy, to be sent county auditor by district clerk ............... 42
of election, to vote upon erection or removal of a school house .... 42
of tax levy, by clerk ............................................................... 51

## OATH

county superintendent has power to administer ......................... 27
of office, to be taken by members of board of education ....... 78, 111
to be taken by judges and clerks of election ............................. 36
judges and clerks of election, have power to administer, when .... 36
of office, to be taken by directors and treasurer ....................... 37
of district officers, where to be filed ....................................... 39

## OFFICE

of state superintendent, where to be held ................................ 13
of county superintendent to be provided by county commissioners ..... 28
expenses of, to be paid by county ...................................... 28, 29

## OFFICERS

(See District School Officers.)

## ORAL INSTRUCTION

to be given in physiology and hygiene, and effects of alcoholic drinks.. 60

## ORGANIZATION

of new school district, how made ............................................ 31
of special district ................................................................... 70
of board of education .............................................................. 72
of district school boards, how effected .................................... 37
of schools, by district board ............................................... 40, 43

## PENALTY

for failure of treasurer to give additional bonds ....................... 38
for failure to make proper indorsement on unpaid warrants ....... 66
for willful disturbance of public schools ................................... 66
for not sending children to school ..................................... 63, 64
president of board, for not prosecuting .................................... 64
for employing any children between 8 and 14 years of age ........ 64
of school officers for neglect of duty ....................................... 65
for false election returns ........................................................ 65

**PENALTY—Continued.**

of treasurer for failure to pay over funds .................................... 65, 66
for removing school house furniture.................................... 42
for trespass upon school lands.................................... 136
(See Fines, Forfeitures and Penalties.)

**PERMANENT SCHOOL FUND**

what constitutes permanent school fund.................................... 9, 10, 15
to remain inviolate.................................... 15
state to make good losses of .................................... 15
interest and income of, to be apportioned to common schools............ 15, 16
how to be invested.................................... 18

**PETITION**

of one-third of voters required to call meeting to vote bonds.............. 67
of residents for a new school district .................................... 30, 31
for special district.................................... 71
for the erection of a school house.................................... 42
for a school, by parents or guardians .................................... 43
for vote to adopt free text books .................................... 90

**PHYSIOLOGY AND HYGIENE**

to be taught to all pupils.................................... 60

**PLATS**

of county to be made by county auditor.................................... 34

**POLLING PLACES**

how established.................................... 35
when open .................................... 35

**POWERS, RIGHTS AND DUTIES**

of school corporations.................................... 34
of special districts.................................... 71
of board of education in special districts.................................... 73
of district board to furnish schools.................................... 40
of district board to furnish supplies to schools.................................... 40
of district board to employ teachers.................................... 41
of district to admit pupils from other districts .................................... 41
of district board to make rules.................................... 41
of district board to determine branches of study.................................... 41
of district board to levy tax .................................... 42
of district board to have charge of school house.................................... 42

**PROFESSIONAL CERTIFICATE**

.................................... 55

**PROPERTY**

minimum of in school district.................................... 31
subject to taxation in special districts.................................... 75

**PUBLIC INSTITUTIONS**

location of .................................... 19
grants of land to.................................... 19, 20
similar ones not to be located, except by revision of constitution......... 20

**PUBLIC LANDS**

proceeds from sale of, to make permanent school fund.................................... 15

**PUBLIC SCHOOLS**

to be provided .................................... 9
to be open to all children.................................... 9
to be free from sectarian control .................................... 9

PUBLIC SCHOOLS—Continued.

    provision to be made for, by legislative assembly............................ 15

    to be free from the primary to the collegiate course........................ 15

    what instruction to be given in............................................... 15

PUPILS

    when may be suspended....................................................... 41, 60

    assignment of studies to..................................................... 60

    may be sent to a school out of the district, when......,.................... 41

QUALIFICATIONS

    of state superintendent...................................................... 13, 23

    of county superintendent..................................................... 29

    of voters and school officers................................................ 35

    of teachers.................................................................. 57, 58

QUESTIONS

    for examinations, prepared by state superintendent......................... 24, 55

QUORUM

    of board of education in special districts................................... 72

    of district school board, necessary for transaction of business............. 37

READING CIRCLES

    fee for professional and normal certificates, to be used for................ 56

    duties of county superintendent in relation thereto......................... 26, 27

REAL PROPERTY

    of school district, how chosen and obtained................................. 42, 43

RECORD

    of bonds to be kept by clerk................................................ 67

    of cancelled bonds to be kept by clerk.......................................69

    of visits to schools, and all official acts to be kept by county super-

        intendent.............................................................. 26, 27

RECORDS

    to be preserved and open to inspection...................................... 45

    to be kept in English language............................................... 45

    to be preserved by state superintendent..................................... 23

    to be kept by county superintendent......................................... 027

REGISTERS

    to be furnished by state department......................................... 24, 40

    teachers to keep............................................................ 59

RENT

    of school lands, how paid................................................... 134, 135

REPAIRS

    of school houses to be made by district board............................... 40

REPORT

    teacher to make, in duplicate, at end of term............................... 59

    teacher's, one copy be filed with district clerk, one to be sent to county

        superintendent......................................................... 59

    county superintendent to make to state superintendent, when................. 28

    clerk of board of education to make, of enumeration......................... 45

    to be made by special districts, when....................................... 74

    clerk of district to make to county superintendent annually................. 45

    clerk's annual to be examined by district board............................. 45

    copies of district clerk's to be filed in his office and another to be sent to

        county superintendent.................................................. 45

    to be preserved for examination, how........................................ 45

    state superintendent to make, when.......................................... 25

    of state superintendent, to be printed, when, and distributed, how.......... 25

    of district treasurer, when to be made...................................... 48, 49

    county superintendent to report institute fund on hand...................... 61

RETURNS

    how canvassed in special districts.......................................... 77

    of votes at annual elections, how made...................................... 36

S. L.—13.

## REVOCATION
of state certificate .......................................................... 56
of county certificate.......................................................... 58
when county superintendent should revoke certificate.................... 28

## RIGHTS
(See Powers, Rights and Duties.)

## RULES
board to assist teacher in making.......................................... 41
pertaining to appeals to be prescribed by state superintendent of public
instruction.................................................................... 24
for management of academy of science...................................... 106
for management of agricultural college .................................... 109

## SALARY AND FEES
of state superintendent...................................................... 13, 25
of county superintendent..................................................... 28, 29
of county superintendent in leasing and sale of school lands............ 28
of school directors........................................................... 37
of district clerk............................................................. 37
of school treasurer........................................................... 39
for leasing school lands ..................................................... 124, 126

## SALE OF SCHOOL LANDS
how made...................................................................... 124, 125
lands to be designated for.................................................... 124
hours for .................................................................... 124
terms of ..................................................................... 125
expenses, how paid............................................................ 122
advertisement of ............................................................. 124
when void..................................................................... 126, 128

## SATURDAY
teacher not to be permitted to teach on...................................... 59

## SCHOOLS
management of, by district board ............................................. 40
to be established by district board .......................................... 40
who may be employed to teach in ............................................. 41
when pupils may be suspended from ........................................... 41
pupils from other districts may be admitted to, when...................... 41
what branches of study to be taught in....................................... 41, 60
when new schools must be organized........................................... 43
terms of, how arranged—additional terms, when allowed................... 43, 44
when may be discontinued...................................................... 43, 44
general supervision of, by state superintendent............................ 23
supervision of by county superintendent .................................... 26
(See Public Schools and Common Schools.)

## SCHOOL AGE
what is ...................................................................... 63

## SCHOOL BOARD
(See District School Board.)

## SCHOOL CALENDAR
.............................................................................. 148

## SCHOOL DISTRICTS
what shall constitute district school corporation.......................... 30
boundaries of school district to conform with civil township, where
possible...................................................................... 30
what territory may be organized into district school corporations........ 30, 31
new school districts, how formed............................................. 31
when school districts may be divided and attached to other districts.... 31
how district system may be changed to township, when..................... 31
parts of three or more districts may be consolidated into a separate school
district ..................................................................... 31

## SCHOOL DISTRICTS—Continued.

when civil township may consolidate into school district .................... 32
name of school district ..................................................... 32
boundaries of district (in district counties), how to be arranged and
   established ...................................................... 32, 33
boundaries, how changed in future ....................................... 33
rights and powers of school corporations ................................ 34
plats of school districts to be filed ...................................... 34
state tuition fund to be apportioned to, how ............................ 48
bonds, how may be issued ............................................. 66, 67
prohibited from making certain gifts and loans ......................... 19

## SCHOOL FUNDS

state tuition fund, how raised .......................................... 46
county treasurer to report to state auditor ............................. 46
state superintendent to apportion state tuition fund to counties ....... 46
funds defined ........................................................... 47
funds controlled and paid out by district treasurer .................... 47
county treasurer to furnish state auditor statement ................... 47
apportionment of funds by county superintendent ..................... 48
treasurer's accounts, how kept ....................................... 47, 48
county treasurer to pay over funds to district treasurer, when ......... 49
to keep account with school corporation ............................... 50
not to be loaned or used for any private purpose ...................... 65
permanent school fund ..................................... 9, 10, 15, 46

## SCHOOL HOUSES

proposals for building .................................................. 69
bonds may be voted to meet indebtedness for .......................... 70
when may be used for other than school purposes ..................... 42
sites for, how selected and obtained ................................. 42, 43
when may be built ...................................................... 42
when may be moved .................................................... 42

## SCHOOL LANDS

how may be sold and leased ..................................... 9, 10, 15
to be disposed of as legislature provides .............................. 11
terms on which to be sold ............................................. 16
when to be subject to taxation ......................................... 17
how to be advertised for sale ......................................... 17
patent for, when to issue .............................................. 17
when may be sold ...................................................... 17
claims for improvements on, not to be recognized ..................... 18
(See University and School Lands.)
(See Trespass upon School Lands.)

## SCHOOL LIBRARY

(See Library.)

## SCHOOL LAW

when to be printed .................................................... 24

## SCHOOL OF MINES

lands granted for .................................................. 11, 19
where located ......................................................... 19

## SCHOOL WEEK

defined ................................................................. 59

## SCHOOL YEAR

defined ................................................................. 59

## SEAL

state superintendent to have .......................................... 24

## SECRETARY OF STATE

member of board of university and school lands ................... 16, 119

## SECTARIAN
Bible not deemed—reading of optional with pupil........................ 61
public schools to be free from the control of.................... ................ 9, 15
schools not to receive public money........................................... 15
schools not to receive proceeds of sale of lands............................. 10

## SETTLEMENT
district board to make annually with treasurer............. ................. 48, 49

## SITE
for school house, how selected................ .............................. 42
may be taken without consent of owner, how.. ........................... 43

## SPECIAL DISTRICTS
entitled to proportion state tuition fund..................,.......... 48
what cities governed by the provisions of............................... 70
how organized...................................................... 71
election of board of education................................... 72
terms of office of board, quorum................................... 72
meetings of board.................................................. 72
members not to be interested in school contracts....................... 72
annual and special meetings of the board........................... 72
organization of the board.......................................... 72
duties of president................................................ 72
duties of clerk.................................................... 73
powers and duties of board........ ................................ 73
board to make reports.............................................. 74
moneys to be paid over to treasurer of district.... ................ 74
supervision of schools of special district........................... 74
taxable property.................................................. 75
annual school tax levy, to be made by board of education............. ... 75
expenditures—contracts, how to be made.......................... 75
treasurer of district, who shall be............................... 75
duties of treasurer, bond required of.......... ................ ........ 75
equalization of school debts and property........................... 76
when special district may dissolve................................ 76
election of boards of education in special districts.................. 76
when adjacent territory may be added to special district ............... 70
name and power of special district................................ 71
conveyance of property to, how.................................... 71
notice of election, precincts—canvass of returns, how made........... 77
certificates of election........................................... 77
vacancies, how filled—oath........................................ 78
bonds, how and when may be issued................................ 78
bond election, what bonds to specify............................. 78, 79
tax levy for interest and sinking fund.............................. 79
investment of sinking fund........................................ 79
interest of bonds, how paid—security for bonds, what.................. 79
bond register..................................................... 80
power of board to issue bonds to refund outstanding bonds ............. 80
unused funds may be transferred.................................. 80
(See Independent School Districts.)

## SPECIAL LAWS
passage of by legislature prohibited... ............................. 13
what special laws in force and effect............. .................... 139

## SPECIAL MEETINGS
of board of education in special districts......................... 72

## SPECULATION
in office prohibited........................................ 140

## STATE AUDITOR

member of the board of university and school lands................ 10, 119
to certify state tuition fund to state superintendent.................... 46
to pay bills of institute conductors, when........................ 62
to issue warrants for expenses of board of university and school land-.. 122, 138

## STATE'S ATTORNEYS

to report trespassers upon school lands and prosecute same.............. 137

## STATE SUPERINTENDENT OF PUBLIC INSTRUCTION

(See Superintendent of Public Instruction.)

## STATE TREASURER

to demand of county treasurers state tuition fund.................... 46
to forward apportionment of state tuition fund to county treasurers.... 46, 47
duties of, in relation to state tuition fund.......................... 46, 47
member of board of trustees........................................ 105
custodian of funds for academy of science ......................... 107
custodian of funds derived from sale and lease of university and school
lands ...................................................... 121
duties of, in relation to funds of normal schools.................... 102

## STATE TUITION FUND

how acquired............................................... 15, 16, 46
to be apportioned to common schools.......... .................. 16
special districts entitled to their proportion of............ .. ......... 48
how apportioned............................................. 46, 48
amount in county treasury to be reported to state auditor............. 46
defined ....................................................... 47
certain taxes to be added to ................................... 51
to be used only in payment of teachers' wages.................... 47
in case insufficient to pay teachers' wages........................ 47
in case more than sufficient to pay teachers' wages................ 47

## SUPERINTENDENT OF PUBLIC INSTRUCTION

election, qualification, term of office............................. 13, 23
to preserve miscellaneous documents............................. 23
ex-officio member of the board of university and school lands........... 21, 119
ex-officio member state normal school boards........................ 23
to furnish school supplies....................................... 23
to prepare teachers' certificates, questions for examination, etc........ 24
to prepare and prescribe course of study for public schools........... 24
to prescribe rules for teachers' institutes, appoint conductors, etc....... 24
to advise county superintendents, decide appeals, etc................. 24
record of official acts.......................................... 24
school laws to be printed....................................... 24
conference with county superintendents............................ 24
seal ........................................................ 24
to assist at teachers' institutes.................................. 25
biennial report, what to contain, number and distribution of.......... 25
salary and traveling expenses................................... 25
duties in relation to plats of school districts...................... 34
vacancy, how filled........................................... 53
to prepare examination questions............................... 55
re-examination of papers of applicants for county certificates, when.... 57
duties of, in relation to institutes.............................. 61, 62
to apportion state tuition fund to counties........................ 46
to apportion expenses of county conductors of institutes............. 61
ex-officio member of board of directors for normal schools............ 101
office of, where to be held..................................... 13
salary of................................................... 13, 25
to furnish registers and blanks................................ 40
to approve bills of institute conductors, when..................... 62
to prescribe rules and regulations pertaining to appeals............. 24
member of board of trustees.................................... 105
secretary of board of university and school lands................... 23, 119

## SUPERINTENDENT OF SCHOOLS
(See County Superintendent of Schools.)

## SUPREME COURT
(See Decisions of Supreme Court.)

## SUSPENSION OF PUPILS

when may be allowed............................................................. 41, 60

## TAXES

school taxes, how and when collected................................ 50, 51
levy to be made by school board.......................................... 42, 50
notice of levy to be sent to county auditor by district clerk.............. 51
county auditor's duty in relation thereto.................................... 51
how levied.................................................................. 51
maximum levy for final judgment, taxes to be uniform................. 51
statement of assessed valuation, to be made by assessor................. 52
adjustment of indebtedness of district in case of illegal board, or of
    failure to elect board................................................. 52
equalization to be arrived at by arbitration.............................. 54
to equalize and pay previous debt........................................ 54
maximum tax for all sch ol purposes..................................... 55
to meet indebtedness, to be assessed before debt incurred............... 10
in special district, annual levy of, to be made by board................. 75
to be levied by school board, when....................................... 42
may be levied by board in independent school districts.................. 83, 84

## TAXATION

when school lands to be subject to....................................... 17, 130

## TEACHERS

duty of in relation to reading circles.................................... 26, 27
examination for professional or normal certificate....................... 55, 56
examination for county certificate....................................... 56
qualifications of.......................................................... 57, 58
residence and citizenship................................................. 58
given opportunity to make defense in proceedings to revoke certificate... 58
to give notice of opening and closing school.............................. 59
not entitled to compensation when teaching without a certificate........ 59
may teach six weeks after certificate has expired by its own limitation... 59
to keep a register and make report at close of term....................... 59
last month's wages not to be paid until term report is made.............. 59
required to attend county institute...................................... 60
how employed.............................................................. 41
contract with, to be in writing.......................................... 41
when may be dismissed..................................................... 41
relatives of board ineligible in certain cities........................... 89
(See Duties of Teachers.)

## TERM OF OFFICE

of county superintendent.................................................. 26
of board of education in special districts................................ 72
of directors.............................................................. 34
of district treasurer..................................................... 34
of superintendent of public instruction.................................. 23

## TERMS OF SCHOOL

length required........................................................... 43
additional time, when allowed............................................. 44

## TEXT BOOKS
(See Free Text Books.)

## TIMBER

on school lands, not to be destroyed...................................... 135

TOWN OR VILLAGE
how may be consolidated into one district.................................. 31

TREASURER
(See District Treasurer.)

TREASURER OF SPECIAL DISTRICT
to receive moneys belonging to the district............................... 74
who shall be........................................................... 75
duties of.............................................................. 75
required to give bond.................................................. 75

TREASURER OF INDEPENDENT DISTRICTS
custodian of moneys, and general duties................................ 85
bond................................................................... 85

TRESPASS UPON SCHOOL LANDS
penalty for........................................................ 136, 137
who held to be guilty of............................................... 136
duties of state's attorneys............................................ 137
duty of attorney general.............................................. 137
property to be seized................................................. 137
defense and suits.................................................... 137
damages for......................................................... 137

UNCULTIVATED LANDS
not to be broken by lessee............................................ 135

UNIVERSITY AND SCHOOL LANDS, LEASE AND SALE OF
board of, how constituted............................................. 119
authority............................................................. 120
meetings of board.................................................... 120
authority to invest funds.............................................. 120
records of............................................................ 121
state treasurer custodian of funds..................................... 121
state treasurer to collect moneys...................................... 121
term of office of commissioner........................................ 122
appraisal for sale..................................................... 123
selecting for sale..................................................... 124
advertisement of...................................................... 124
manner of............................................................ 124
terms of.............................................................. 125
adjournment of....................................................... 125
withdrawn lands...................................................... 125
approval of sale................................................... 125, 126
execution of contracts of.............................................. 126
void sales......................................................... 126, 128
surveys of............................................................ 126
subdivision into small tracts.......................................... 127
new appraisal........................................................ 127
map of............................................................... 127
contract, effect of.................................................... 127
assignee of purchasers................................................ 127
sale void on failure to pay interest, principal or taxes................. 128
redemption before re-sale............................................. 128
fee in state until patents are issued................................... 129
reconveyance to United States......................................... 129
patents, when to issue................................................ 129
patents to be recorded................................................ 130
taxation of lands sold................................................. 130
duty of county auditor............................................. 130, 131
duty of county treasurer........................................... 130, 131
commissioner to furnish county treasurer with list of lands sold........ 131
township assessors to examine lands................................... 132

## UNIVERSITY AND SCHOOL LANDS, LEASE AND SALE OF—Continued.

quantity of lands to be sold........................................................ 132
subject to lease...................................................................... 132
appraisement for lease.............................................................. 132
selection of lands for lease......................................................... 133
advertisement for lease............................................................. 133
manner of leasing.................................................................... 134
deposit by bidders, forfeit on failure to pay..................................... 134
adjournment of lease................................................................ 134
approval of lease and execution of contract for................................. 135
lessee not to destroy timber........................................................ 135
lessee not to break uncultivated lands............................................ 135
hay not to be cut before July 10th................................................. 136
permits to cut hay and to remove dead and down timber....................... 136
board to appoint agents.............................................................. 136
civil action for trespass.............................................................. 136
willful trespass....................................................................... 136
penalty for trespass.................................................................. 136
defense and suits..................................................................... 137
expenses for advertising for lease and sale....................................... 137
appropriation for expenses of board............................................... 138

## UNIVERSITY OF NORTH DAKOTA

where located........................................................................ 19, 94
lands granted for..................................................................... 10, 11
board of trustees, how appointed................................................. 94
powers and duties—meetings...................................................... 94, 95
report—powers of trustees.......................................................... 95, 96
powers of president and faculty.................................................... 96
object and departments of university.............................................. 96
course of instruction................................................................. 97
pupils who may become.............................................................. 97
tuition fees........................................................................... 98
compensation of trustees............................................................ 98
law library for........................................................................ 99
loan of muskets for.................................................................. 99
Scandinavian language taught...................................................... 97

## VACANCIES

in office of superintendent of public instruction, how filled................... 53
county superintendent, how filled................................................. 53
director, how filled.................................................................. 53
district treasurer, how filled....................................................... 38, 53
district clerk, how filled............................................................ 53
in board of education, in special districts, how filled........................... 78
in treasurer's office, when.......................................................... 38

## VISITATION OF SCHOOLS

by county superintendent........................................................... 26
by members of board of education, in independent districts.................... 86

## VOTES

how canvassed at annual election.................................................. 36

## WARRANTS

when properly drawn, to be paid by treasurer.................................... 38
to be endorsed, how—when not paid.............................................. 38
what to specify....................................................................... 39

## WOMEN

entitled to vote, when............................................................... 14
qualified to vote and hold school office........................................... 35

www.ingramcontent.com/pod-product-compliance
Lightning Source LLC
Chambersburg PA
CBHW020540270326
41927CB00006B/660